THE SHEPHERD'S HEART

Hope for a Broken Society

ALAN JAMES SCHRADER

The Shepherd's Heart: Hope for a Broken Society
Copyright © 2024 by Dr. Alan James Schrader
Published by Engage Ministries
25595 Chardon Road
Cleveland, OH 44143
www.AlanJamesSchrader.com
Drajschrader@gmail.com

Cover Design by Rachel Schrader
Edited by Edie Mourey
First Edition: July 2024
Printed in the United States of America
ISBN: 9798653679827

All rights reserved. No part of this book may be reproduced, scanned, or distributed in any printed or electronic form without permission.

Unless indicated all Scripture quotations are from the New King James Version of the Bible. Copyright © 1779, 1980, 1982, Thomas Nelson Inc., Publisher. Used by permission.

Scripture quotations marked (NLT) are taken from the Holy Bible, New Living Translation, copyright ©1996, 2004, 2015 by Tyndale House Foundation. Used by permission of Tyndale House Publishers, a Division of Tyndale House Ministries, Carol Stream, Illinois 60188. All rights reserved.

Scripture quotations marked (MSG) are taken from The Message, copyright © 1993, 2002, 2018 by Eugene H. Peterson. Used by permission of NavPress. All rights reserved. Represented by Tyndale House Publishers.

DEDICATION

Dedicated to Mary J. Schrader

Mary, you are my best friend and beloved wife. Thank you for being at my side these last thirty-plus years. We've rejoiced together, cried together, prayed together, and worshipped our Lord and Savior together. Thank you also for being a loving and faithful mother and grandmother to our beautiful children and grandchildren. I will forever be grateful for the gift God has given me through you.

I love you forever. I love you always.
Your Alan James

CONTENTS

Acknowledgments	vii
Foreword	ix
Introduction	1
1. He Makes Me	15
Let's Think About It	35
A Courageous Prayer	37
2. He Leads Me	39
Let's Think About It	61
A Courageous Prayer	63
3. He Restores Me	65
Let's Think About It	81
A Courageous Prayer	83
4. He Guides Me	85
Let's Think About It	105
A Courageous Prayer	107
5. He Is With Me	109
Let's Think About It	125
A Courageous Prayer	127
6. He Prepares Me	129
Let's Think About It	145
A Courageous Prayer	147
7. He Anoints Me	149
Let's Think About It	169
A Courageous Prayer	171
8. He Follows Me	173

Let's Think About It	197
A Courageous Prayer	199
Conclusion	201
Appendix	205
References	215
About the Author	219
Also by Dr. Alan James Schrader	221

ACKNOWLEDGMENTS

History records Winston Churchill saying, "Writing a book is an adventure." I would have to agree as writing this book has recalled over thirty years of my adventure in pastoral ministry.

There have been many in those years who have greatly impacted my life, and I want especially to acknowledge some of the individuals who have mentored me. These men and women have demonstrated outstanding character and compassion in their ministries. They have marked my life as I have observed their lives, some from a distance and others up close. Half on my list have gone on to their reward; the other half, I continue to watch from a distance and learn. That being said, I wish to express my gratitude to the following men and women, my mentors, whose pastoral love and care have personally blessed my life:

- Pastor Joe & Josephine Pileggi, Sr.
- Pastor Nick & Irene Welch
- Pastor George & Ruth Veach
- Pastor Hubert & Harriet Bunny
- Pastor Richard & Donna Brockway
- Pastor Bob & Ruby Smallman
- Pastor Doug & Patty Cowburn
- Pastor Al & Karen Hamm
- Pastor Bob & Marci Sorge
- Pastor Chester & Mary Ruth Gretz
- Pastor Bernard & Sharon Evans
- Pastor Michael & Mary Marino

With *all* my heart, thank you!

FOREWORD

What a wonderful privilege it is to have Jesus Christ as the Shepherd of our lives. He meets our needs, orders our steps, guides us, and watches over our lives continually.

Many seek the things that can only be sufficiently found in the Good Shepherd. The word *good* carries within it the idea of something beautiful, noble, and blameless. Many great men in the Scriptures were shepherds, but none greater than Jesus Christ, the Son of God.

In the Old Testament, the sheep died for the shepherd, but under the New Covenant, the Shepherd died for the sheep. Jesus willingly gave

His life for the sheep, and now He shepherds us all of our days with His loving and perfect care.

The Good Shepherd knows His sheep personally and intimately. He knows our names, our natures, and, of course, our needs. That is why Psalm 23 is such a comfort and strength to the believer. Though often read at funerals, Psalm 23 is a message that applies to the days of our lives right now (see Psalm 23:6).

Such good news is found in this moving psalm as we realize the Savior who died for us also lives for us and cares for us the way a shepherd cares for his sheep (see John 10). If you can say, "The Lord is my Shepherd," you can also say, "I shall not want."

The Good Shepherd died for the sheep, and the Great Shepherd lives for the sheep—to protect them, provide for them, and direct them. The Good Shepherd gave His life *to* the sheep, and the Great Shepherd gave His life *for* the sheep. In our Shepherd, we have eternal life *and* abundant life. In Him, we find security, significance, and salvation.

Pastor Alan Schrader has done an excellent job expounding on the role of the Good Shepherd and

His great care for His sheep. With rich insights into the ministry of the Shepherd, mixed with many moving and personal testimonies from his own life, Pastor Schrader reveals and encourages us to receive the matchless ministry that only Jesus Christ offers and desires to give to each of us. Pastor Alan helps us see the heart of Jesus and how His ministry as a shepherd is so important for every one of us.

You will find this book both insightful and inspirational. I recommend it for both individual growth and group study.

Pastor Joe Zaino
Pleasant Grove Assembly of God Church
Plant City, Florida

INTRODUCTION

The LORD is my shepherd; I shall not want.

PSALM 23:1

Psalm 23 has been memorized and quoted by millions. Even non-religious people have been exposed to and taken solace in the words of this beautiful psalm. The chapter begins, however, with this one essential criteria: *Only those who allow the Lord to be their Shepherd can claim, "I shall not want."*

Sadly, today, we live in a society that has lost its way and is filled with want. In its primitive root, the Hebrew word for *want* means to lack and, by implication, to fail, lessen, or be in want. It also means to be diminished, bereaved, decreased, (have) lack, and made lower.

What does our society need so that it no longer wants but instead experiences provision, comfort, and healing? Our society needs to know the Good Shepherd—that's what we all need.

We live in a world that seemingly has so much to offer us yet, in truth, has so little. Not only do the homeless in our major cities go without, but even people with great wealth experience lack in their lives. These can live without knowing their purpose or experiencing love and contentment, resulting in their asking themselves existential questions like, *Why am I here? Where did I come from? Where am I going?* These are valid and essential questions that strike at the heart of those who are increasingly fearful of facing what appears to be a despairing and threatening future.

On top of everything else, people are loaded down with feelings of shame, guilt, emptiness, and rejection. Many run to mental health centers and prescription counters for relief, only to find that legitimate drugs are not much more effective than illegitimate ones, and may do just as much damage in the long run. We have become a generation of drug users for any and all occasions, yet we still suffer from depression and hopelessness.

Though medical science and technology continue to extend life on earth, war, crime, rage, hate, murder, disease, and fear devastate our society. Our news headlines are replete with riots, shootings, and suicides—all manner of violence and destruction. Furthermore, we are all painfully aware of what our political or governmental leaders give as answers for creating a "better" society, and what they're offering all falls short of our ideals, never mind meeting the basic requirements of God's Word. The hostility in our modern-day politics is so toxic, in fact, that people are ready to lie, steal, and even kill for their individual political ideology.

The sad truth is a significant portion of our society lives in open and defiant rebellion against God. We see people act as if they have no conscience when it comes to acts of sexual immorality, violence, thievery, or protest.

What kind of insanity has overtaken us? Where are the values and principles of character, integrity, and morality that once held us together as a nation? Why can't we seem to live in peace and harmony with each other? Where does all the hate or desire for vengeance come from?

TWO DREAMS

While writing this book, I had two dreams that I believe are very relevant to what is happening around us, pointing us to the importance of living under the care of the Good Shepherd and not experiencing want. Let me explain.

In the first dream, I saw a female deer, a doe, slowly climb a mountain. The doe was tentative in its gait and gaze, giving me the sense the animal was on high alert. As the doe continued to climb, there came a point at which I could no longer see it, but I could see the trail it had left behind.

As I looked up the mountain, following the trail with my eyes, I suddenly saw a pack of wolves nosing their way up the trail, following the doe's scent. The wolves weren't racing after the doe but walking stealthily, heads lowered, as if wanting to sneak up on their prey, to catch the doe by surprise.

As I watched this whole scene unfold, I began praying. I was then reminded of the scheming and devious planning that takes place in our world today, just as the psalmist declared:

> The kings of the earth set themselves, and the rulers take counsel together, against the LORD and against His Anointed, saying "Let us break their bonds in pieces and cast away their cords from us."
>
> PSALM 2:2–3

I could tell in the dream the wolf pack's plan was to take down the isolated doe and devour it.

The scene soon changed, and I then found myself among other people, whom I was urging to stay alert because of the wolf pack's—the enemy's—schemes that I had witnessed in my dream. I was explicitly aware of the enemy sneaking in and trying to destroy our homes, cities, communities, and churches.

In the second dream, I watched two small animals fight and try to devour one another. The confusing yet alarming thing was that neither animal was big enough to eat the other one. I watched as they made loud noises and tried to inflict wounds on each other, but neither animal took down the other.

Finally, after watching these two small animals spar together for a while, I saw them become so exhausted that they could no longer fight. However, as soon as the animals dropped to the ground to rest, a pack of wolves immediately came and attacked the tiny creatures. Apparently, the wolf pack had heard the commotion the two small animals had made and then came and devoured them both.

After the second dream, I woke up and wrote down what I had just witnessed in both dreams. I thought first of the scripture:

> For all the law is fulfilled in one word, even in this: "You shall love your neighbor as yourself." But if you bite and devour one

another, beware lest you be consumed by one another.

GALATIANS 5:14–15

Upon further thinking about the dreams, I was reminded of recent discussions on news and social media regarding the Russian interference in US elections during the 2016 presidential race. One of the conclusions drawn from Robert Mueller's indictment of the Russian nationals who meddled in the presidential election was that their strategy was to create chaos and confusion in the election polls. Whether we can trust anything in media these days or not, one thing is sure, and it is this: *The enemy of our souls wants to create chaos, confusion, and deception in our world.* Therefore, he plans to steal, kill, and destroy—like the thief Jesus talked about in John 10:10 and the pack of wolves I dreamed about.

THE GOOD SHEPHERD AND HIS SHEEP

John 10 is a beautiful chapter. In it, Jesus provided a great illustration, describing Himself as the *Good Shepherd* and we His people as *His sheep*. He said in verse 9, "I am the door. If anyone enters by Me, he will be saved, and will go in and out and find pasture." It's after this verse, however, that Jesus warned about the thief, and then He warned about a hireling, "who is not the shepherd," neither the owner of the sheep, running away when he "sees the wolf coming" (John 10:11–13). In fact, the hireling's fast departure results in the wolf catching the sheep and scattering them.

What we see in Jesus' illustration is that Satan is indeed after us sheep. Satan wants us scattered and running. He knows that, if we turn away from the reality and knowledge of the Good Shepherd, away from abiding under the Shepherd's watchful care within the Shepherd's secure pastures, it's only a matter of time until we become victims of Satan's attack. It's also only a matter of time until we become wanting like many in our society who don't know the Good Shepherd.

I continue to be aware of people who, rather than being led by the Good Shepherd, spend their time being shepherded by FOX, CNN, MSNBC, ABC, CBS, and other similar news outlets. In

Matthew 7:15, Jesus said, "Beware of false prophets who come to you in sheep's clothing, but inwardly they are ravenous wolves." The heart of the true Shepherd wants to expose these "false prophets" or "ravenous wolves." The apostle Paul spoke about such wolves when he instructed the elders of the church in Ephesus:

> Therefore take heed to yourselves and to all the flock, among which the Holy Spirit has made you overseers, to shepherd the church of God which He purchased with His own blood. For I know this, that after my departure, savage wolves will come in among you, not sparing the flock. Also from among yourselves men will rise up, speaking perverse things, to draw away the disciples after themselves.
>
> ACTS 20:28–30

We are admonished in the Scriptures not to allow Satan to "take advantage of us; for we are not ignorant of his devices" (2 Corinthians 2:11). We cannot forget the voice of the Great Shepherd who desires us not to fail, not to suffer want, nor cease in understanding our meaning or purpose.

I have learned recently about the relationship and interaction of shepherds with their sheep. For example, once in a while, a female sheep or ewe will give birth to a lamb and then reject it. And once a ewe rejects one of its lambs, the ewe will never change its mind. Little lambs that are rejected in this way will hang their heads so low that it looks like something is wrong with their necks. Why do they do this? Because their spirit is broken.

What's interesting is these lambs are called "bummer lambs." Unless the shepherd intervenes, a bummer lamb will die, rejected and alone. So, do you know what the shepherd does with a bummer lamb? He takes that rejected little one into his home, hand-feeds it, and keeps it warm by the fire. He will wrap it with blankets and hold it to his chest so the bummer lamb can hear his heartbeat. Once the lamb is strong enough, the shepherd will place it back in the field with the rest of the flock. But that sheep never forgets how the shepherd cared for it when its mother rejected it. Whenever the shepherd calls for the flock, guess who runs to him first? Yes, it is the bummer lamb. It intimately knows the shepherd's voice. The bummer lamb isn't necessarily loved more; it simply believes it *is* loved more by the shepherd because it has experienced the shepherd one-on-one.

You see, many of us are like bummer lambs, rejected and broken. But the Lord is the Good Shepherd. He cares for our every need and holds us close to His heart so we can hear His heartbeat. We may experience brokenness, but the Good Shepherd profoundly loves us. He will be faithful to comfort us and bring us home.

When Jesus presented Himself in John 10:11 as the Good Shepherd, He was not just representing Himself. He had been commissioned by the Father to do the work given to Him and minister the doctrine and teaching entrusted to Him. Jesus was being, doing, and saying as the Father showed and told Him so that, when people saw Him, they saw the Father (see John 5:19; John 14:7, 9). If they rejected Jesus, then they also rejected the Father.

Jesus' vital connection to the Father is significant for us to understand because it shows us the heart of the Father, the heart of the Great Shepherd, is to bring hope to a broken people and world—to seek and save the lost (see Luke 19:10).

As our Good Shepherd, then, Jesus understands:

- We all need green pastures.
- We all need still waters.
- We all need restoration.
- We all need guidance.
- We all need His presence.
- We all need a vision of His eternal plan.
- We all need His anointing.
- We all need a revelation of His goodness and mercy.

Jesus followed all the principles of a good shepherd when He came to the earth. He came with a purpose. Jesus knew His Father's business was establishing the Church amid a broken society. He knew that humanity would continue to be in want without the Shepherd's heart to tend to us. Because of the Father's great love for the world, He sent His Son, the Good Shepherd (see

John 3:16). And that's who we need today. The Good Shepherd is the answer to our society's and culture's brokenness, and He is the answer to the Church's needs. He is the answer to our needs as well. I believe we desperately need to focus all our attention once more on Jesus as our Good Shepherd.

In the chapters ahead, then, we will more closely examine just how the Shepherd's heart provides for us His sheep so that we don't find ourselves wanting. After each chapter, you will find a section titled "Let's Think about It" with some questions for further consideration. Immediately following this, you will see a "Courageous Prayer" section that's meant as a way for you to engage in prayer with the Shepherd. There's even a place for you to write your own prayer after having read the chapter.

It's my hope that what you read in this book encourages and strengthens you. As you take the time to revisit a very familiar passage of Scripture, may you receive what you need and what the Shepherd has prepared for you. May this book serve as a tool to help you shepherd others in our broken world, leading them to the Great Shepherd of the sheep, the Lord Jesus. And, finally, may this intercessory cry of the psalmist David rise within your heart as you learn more about our Shepherd: "Save Your people, and bless Your inheritance; shepherd them also, and bear them up forever" (Psalm 28:9).

ONE
HE MAKES ME

He makes me to lie down in green pastures. . . .

PSALM 23:2

I grew up in an Upstate New York town called Herkimer. The name comes from an American Patriot Militia Brigadier General called Nicholas Herkimer (1728–1777). History teaches us that General Herkimer died of his wounds after the Battle of Oriskany, which was known as one of the bloodiest battles in the northern theater of the American Revolutionary

War. It is said that, as General Herkimer turned his horse to see the action, he was struck by a ball (gunshot), which shattered his leg and killed his horse. He was then carried by several of his officers to a beech tree, where his men urged him to retreat from further danger. To that, he is reported to have defiantly replied, "I will face the enemy," and calmly sat leaning against the tree and giving directions and encouragement to the men nearby. Historians say this 49-year-old general was determined to keep his men from being discouraged and retreating from the battle, even after being wounded.

I believe some of General Herkimer's characteristics have helped me understand the Shepherd's heart in Psalm 23. For example, the Good Shepherd desires His people to fulfill their purpose in life. Like the general, the Shepherd encourages the sheep, individually and corporately, to push forward and keep marching on. The principle is clear: *Good leaders provide physical and emotional support to those they lead.*

A PSALM OF DAVID

The Twenty-Third Psalm is known as a psalm of David, and in it, David wrote about his experience during his early years caring for sheep (see 1 Samuel 16:10–11). David understood that sheep depend entirely on the shepherd for provision, guidance, and protection. God was like a shepherd to David, and David was like a sheep to God. Yet, throughout the Scriptures, the Lord is presented as a shepherd to His people. The idea begins as early as the book of Genesis, where Moses called the Lord, "the Shepherd, the Stone of Israel" (Genesis 49:24). Other examples of this in the Old Testament include:

- "Save Your people, and bless Your inheritance; shepherd them also, and bear them up forever" (Psalm 28:9).

- "He will feed His flock like a shepherd; He will gather the lambs with His arm, and carry them in His bosom, and gently lead those who are with young" (Isaiah 40:11).

- "And I will give you shepherds according to My heart, who will feed you with knowledge and understanding" (Jeremiah 3:15).

- "'Awake, O sword, against My Shepherd, against the Man who is My Companion [meaning Jesus],' says the LORD of hosts. 'Strike the Shepherd, and the sheep will be scattered'" (Zechariah 13:7).

- "Shepherd Your people with Your staff, the flock of Your heritage, who dwell solitarily in a woodland, in the midst of Carmel; let them feed in Bashan and Gilead, as in days of old" (Micah 7:14).

David understood that the Shepherd *makes* His sheep lie down. He contents and quiets them wherever their journey leads. And their souls dwell at ease in Him as they enjoy green pastures.

Whether we look at General Herkimer or King David, we see a leader who endures when others quit from exhaustion. David, for example, returned home one day with his men from a military expedition to find their homes burned, their families missing, and all their belongings stolen (see 1 Samuel 30:6–20). David's military leaders were disheartened, but David received a word from the Lord to pursue the enemy.

David's six hundred men had fought for several weeks, and they were already tired, but they followed David anyway. Along the way, two hundred men were too exhausted to cross the ravine to engage the enemy, but four hundred men received strength from God to keep going forward. God raised up David, a shepherd boy who understood God's passion, to lead his men to overcome.

PASSION

The Lord not only desires to be our Shepherd so we don't want, but He also is passionate about our enjoying green pastures. Often, He has to *make us* rest and enjoy those pastures.

W. Philip Keller in *A Shepherd Looks at Psalm 23* writes that sheep do not lie down easily and will not unless four conditions are met.[1] Because they are timid, they will not lie down if they are afraid. Because they are social animals, they will not lie down if there is friction among the sheep. If flies or parasites trouble them, they will not lie down. Finally, if sheep are hungry or anxious about food, they will not lie down.

Rest, then, only comes to the sheep when the shepherd has dealt with fear, friction, flies, and famine.[2] It is the Great Shepherd who *makes us* lie down in green pastures.

The New Testament calls Jesus the *Good Shepherd* in John 10:11, as I said previously. Hebrews 13:20 refers to Him as the *Great Shepherd,* and 1 Peter 5:4 refers to Jesus as the *Chief Shepherd.* Each of these titles describe the passion of our Lord. We read in the Gospel of John,

> "As the Father knows Me, even so I know the Father; and I lay down My life for the sheep. And other sheep I have which are

---

1. W. Philip Keller, *A Shepherd Looks at Psalm 23* (Grand Rapids, MI: Zondervan, 2007).
2. Ibid.

not of this fold; them also I must bring, and they will hear My voice; and there will be one flock and one shepherd."

JOHN 10:15–16

Jesus laid down His physical life to give us eternal life. The ultimate expression of passion can be identified in the actions of Jesus Christ, who died for sinful man. As the apostle Paul stated in Romans 5:8, "But God demonstrates His own love toward us, in that while we were still sinners, Christ died for us." The prophet Isaiah foretold Jesus' passion when He declared:

> He was wounded for our transgressions, He was bruised for our iniquities; the chastisement for our peace was upon Him, and by His stripes we are healed. All we like sheep have gone astray; we have turned every one, to his own way; and the LORD has laid on Him the iniquity of us all.

ISAIAH 53:5–6

The Gospels teach us what happened to Jesus leading up to His death. We're told Judas arrived with soldiers and betrayed Jesus with a kiss. Jesus was then arrested. He was forced to walk through a series of false trials where contradicting false witnesses were brought forward to offer false testimony. Despite the absence of any evidence supporting the false claims, Jesus was sentenced to be murdered. He was eventually blindfolded as a mob of cowardly men beat him mercilessly. He was then stripped in great humiliation, and the Bible simply says that they had Him scourged.

Historians tell us that scourging itself was such a painful event that many people died from it without ever making it to their crosses. Historians also explain that Jesus' hands would have been chained above his head to expose his back and legs to an executioner's whip called a *cat o' nine tails* or a *flagrum*. Typically, two men, one on each side, took turns whipping the victim. The whip was a series of long leather straps. At the end of some of the straps were heavy balls of metal intended to tenderize the body of the victim. Some of the straps had hooks made of glass, metal, or bone that would have sunk deeply into the back, shoulders, buttocks, and legs of the victim. Once the hooks had lodged into the tenderized flesh, the executioner would rip the skin, muscle, tendons, and even bones off the victim. The victim's skin and muscles would hang off the body like ribbons as the hooks tore the skin to the nerve layers. The damage could go so deep that even the lungs were bruised, which made breathing difficult. This is what would have been done to Jesus, but His passion didn't stop there.

The pain on the cross and the crucifixion were so horrendous that a word was invented to explain it. It's *excruciating*, which literally means "from the cross." Jesus was affixed to the cross with nails. He suffered horrifically as his death on the cross was prolonged. He agonized, struggling for breath, as death on the cross was a death by asphyxiation. Again, historians tell us that crucified people could end up hanging on the cross for anywhere from hours to days, passing in and out of consciousness as their lungs strained to breathe while laboring under the weight of their bodies. Jesus' crucifixion was a painful and humiliating scene. Hundreds of years before Jesus' death, the prophet Isaiah foresaw it and said:

> He is despised and rejected by men, a Man of sorrows and acquainted with grief. And we hid, as it were, our faces from Him; He was despised, and we did not esteem Him. Surely He has borne our griefs and carried our sorrows; yet we esteemed Him stricken, smitten by God, and afflicted.
>
> ISAIAH 53:3–4

When I think about how passionate Jesus is for us, this is what I think about. I think about all the things Jesus suffered for love. It was in His passion—His death—that He showed His greatest passion for a lost world.

When I think about how passionate Jesus is for us, I also think about His great desire for us to experience His green pastures and the price He paid for us to enjoy those pastures. I also think of the three times Jesus asked Peter after His resurrection, "Do you love Me?" (John 21:15). To which, Peter responded, "Yes, Lord; You know that I love you" (John 21:15). After Peter's response to Jesus, Jesus then said these three things to Peter:

1. "Feed My lambs" (John 21:15).
2. "Tend My sheep" (John 21:16).
3. "Feed My sheep" (John 21:16).

Do you see how passionate Jesus is to see His sheep were and are cared for? Before His arrest, death, and resurrection, Jesus said to Peter, "Satan has asked for you, that he may sift you as wheat. But I have prayed for you, that your faith should not fail; and when you have returned to Me, strengthen your brethren" (Luke 22:31–32). Satan wanted to crush Peter. He hoped to find only chaff and blow it away. But Jesus reassured Peter that his faith would not be destroyed even though it would be compromised. Peter's faith would be renewed, and he would become a leader who showed great passion for the sheep.

PROVISION

I grew up in a home with an Italian mama who always ensured her kids had enough food. I fondly remember going back to my hometown and every time being greeted with the words, "Have you eaten?" Also, while my father was still living, he would always make a special effort to purchase a porterhouse steak and store it in the freezer for when I would come home for a visit. The truth is my parents wanted me to experience green pastures. They showed me the Good Shepherd's heart of provision for His sheep.

The challenge we face in society today is discerning who can lead us to green pastures. We are reminded in the Bible that, in the last days, before Christ's second coming, many questionable and false ministries will appear. False apostles, prophets, evangelists, pastors, and teachers will arise and sow destruction. They will bring divisions and false teachings. In Matthew 24:4–26, Jesus Himself prophesied of their coming:

> Take heed that no one deceives you…. For false christs and false prophets will rise and show great signs and wonders to deceive, if possible, even the elect. See, I have told you beforehand. Therefore if they say to you, "Look, He is in the desert!" do not go out; or "Look, He is in the inner rooms!" do not believe it.

The warning of deceivers in the last days calls for discernment (see Deuteronomy 18:2–22; Revelation 2:2). Every saint should be asking, "What distinguishes healthy ministries from unhealthy and false leadership? And, how do I know the difference?" Discerning will get more challenging in the last days as the push to be relevant to the culture increases pressure for leaders and believers alike to compromise clear biblical values. False ministries often seem more relevant to a culture but offer no real solutions to society's problems. Only the Great Shepherd can lead people into His provision so they don't want, but the problem is many don't recognize the Shepherd and don't know His voice.

Another excellent example of Jesus' desire to provide for His children can be seen in His appearances after He was resurrected. Three times after Jesus was resurrected from the dead, He had fellowship with His disciples around food. The first one is recorded in Luke 24:30, when Jesus met two individuals traveling to Emmaus, a village seven miles from Jerusalem. The travelers eventually invited Jesus into their home. There He ate with them. Verse 30 says, "Now it came to pass, as He sat at the table with them, that He took bread, blessed and broke it, and gave it to them." It's interesting to note the two men finally recognized that it was Jesus who was with them after He had broken the bread.

The second incident regarding food is recorded in Luke 24:41–43:

> But while they still did not believe for joy, and marveled, He said to them, "Have you any food here?" So they gave Him a piece of broiled fish and some honeycomb. And He took it and ate in their presence.

The third account can be seen in John 21:12–14, where we read:

> Jesus said to them, "Come and eat breakfast." Yet none of the disciples dared ask Him, "Who are You?"—knowing that it was the Lord. Jesus then came, took the bread, and gave it to them, and likewise the fish. This is now the third time Jesus showed Himself to His disciples after He was raised from the dead.

What is so interesting to note is that Jesus gave all his guests food. He not only provided it for them and invited them to it, but He Himself divided it among them and put it into their hands. What a beautiful picture of the Shepherd's heart and the great lengths and depths Jesus will go to make us lie down in green pastures. He desires to bring us into a provision that will never disappoint.

PROTECTION

Despite the negative stories we read in the news today, we can all agree that there is nothing more moving than hearing stories of mothers and fathers giving their own lives to save their children. This is a true picture of what the Good Shepherd has done for us, and He continues to protect and defend us, watching over us each and every moment of our lives.

A number of years back, I heard of a Texan mom who died saving her daughter during the Hurricane Harvey flooding. According to authorities, the woman and her daughter drove on a service road and were soon stuck in high water. The mother exited the vehicle with her child. Authorities said she was swept into a canal and floated about a half mile from her vehicle. The 41-year-old mother "absolutely saved the child's life," Officer Carol Riley, a spokeswoman for the Beaumont Police Department, told reporters.[3] "They were in the water for quite some time," Riley said. "When the baby was found, the baby was clinging to her. The mother did her best to keep her child above the water."[4]

What makes a mother put herself in harm's way to save her child? I see it as a picture of the Shepherd's heart to protect and rescue the lambs! It is His love that "bears all things, believes all things, hopes all things, endures all things" (1 Corinthians 13:7).

The Shepherd is our Protector. He will do all He can to keep and save us from harm because He loves us His sheep. But if you'll recall, John 10

---

3. Alexia Fernandez, "Texas Mother Dies Saving Her 3-Year-Old Daughter during Hurricane Harvey Flood: 'The Baby Was Clinging to Her,'" *Yahoo!*, August 29, 2017, https://www.yahoo.com/entertainment/texas-mother-dies-saving-her-023019390.html.
4. Ibid.

mentions someone who is not a true shepherd. And rather than stand up as the defender of the sheep, this individual hightails it and runs when something threatens the wellbeing of the sheep. Nothing is more telling to us about a shepherd or leader than how he or she responds to a threat against the flock of God. False leaders will flee to protect themselves because they're actually hirelings and not real shepherds.

A hireling in biblical times was known as a day laborer. The Greek word *eritheia* originally meant laboring for wages. It was considered a perfectly respectable and responsible thing to do. However, the meaning of the word became defined as something degenerate. In other words, the laborer worked for pay and nothing else as Jesus explained in John 10:12–13:

> But a hireling, he who is not the shepherd, one who does not own the sheep, sees the wolf coming and leaves the sheep and flees; and the wolf catches the sheep and scatters them. The hireling flees because he is a hireling and does not care about the sheep.

The hireling has no motive to protect or to serve. The hireling has only one motivation: "What's in it for me?" In other words, hirelings are completely selfish. Selfishness is when one is concerned primarily with oneself or with one's interests or benefits, regardless of the effect it may have on others. Selfishness makes man focus on what pleases him, even if others suffer or lack protection from the consequences of his choices.

Today, hirelings want a position, not to serve, but to obtain honor, glory, and profit for themselves. They are of a contentious spirit, contending for what it is they can get out of their effort, work, or participation. When someone's goal becomes more important than character, when supposed leaders justify all their actions in the name of a cause, they have begun to degenerate into working for something they want, which has nothing to do with the protection or care they should be offering those whom they lead. They're acting, then, as hirelings.

Almost every Epistle in the New Testament warns of the danger of false prophets and ministries. New Testament writers held nothing back. They exposed false teachers and teachings, going after them in every way they could to protect the flock of God. They described impostors in derogatory and harmful terms. The apostle Peter described the character and ministry methods of false ministers in 2 Peter 2:1–16. And the apostle Paul, in Colossians 2:8 and 16, identified the bitter fruit of false ministries, saying:

> Beware lest anyone cheat you through philosophy and empty deceit, according to the tradition of men, according to the basic principles of the world, and not according to Christ.... So let no one judge you in food or in drink, or regarding a festival or a new moon or sabbaths.

Jesus also compared false ministries to wolves in sheep's clothing. The New Testament described them as "wandering stars," "brute beasts," "blemishes," and "clouds without water" (2 Peter 2:12–13; Jude 1:10, 12–13). Each comparison highlights a dangerous or threatening quality.

The heart of the Good Shepherd, however, is to sound the alarm so that every saint and every church can learn how to discern the spirit of truth from the spirit of error (see 1 John 4:6). Just like consumer advocates alert the public to false advertising, the Shepherd wants to warn believers about false doctrines and false ministries. God wants to reveal His protection because He alone is the Great Shepherd who can make us lie down in green pastures. This warning is the testimony of His unwavering passion, provision, and protection for all our needs.

The Shepherd does not feed us on the stale bread of past experiences, but He gives us fresh supplies every day, like the morning dew and the rising of the sun. And so abundant are they that we lie down among them and are satisfied. This protection is the picture of a happy, joyful, victorious follower of Christ experiencing the Shepherd's heart.

Every man and woman of the Bible fought the battles of life, and those who put their faith in the Good Shepherd became overcomers who experienced green pastures. Hope for our society has everything to do with people experiencing the heart of the Shepherd who shows passion, provision, and protection. Jesus Christ, the Shepherd, is the true Hope for a broken society.

LET'S THINK ABOUT IT

A leader endures when others quit from exhaustion.

FRANK DAMAZIO

Group Discussion: HE MAKES

1. How would you describe the passion of the Great Shepherd?
2. When you think of His provision, what comes to mind?
3. Describe your own need for protection?

A COURAGEOUS PRAYER
HE MAKES ME

Father, I thank You for making me lie down in green pastures. Please help me see that You're calling me to demonstrate Your shepherd's heart to a hurting society. Help me be faithful in revealing Your passion, provision, and protection. I surrender my life in service to You. In the name that is above all other names. Amen!

Write out your prayer today:

TWO
HE LEADS ME

He leads me beside the still waters.

PSALM 23:2

Recently, I had the incredible privilege of attending a School of Nursing graduation ceremony. Before the graduates were about to be recognized as nurses, right before they were "pinned," they were asked to recite the "Florence Nightingale Pledge," saying:

> I solemnly pledge myself before God and in the presence of this assembly, to pass my

life in purity and to practice my profession faithfully. I will abstain from whatever is deleterious and mischievous, and will not take or knowingly administer any harmful drug. I will do all in my power to maintain and elevate the standard of my profession, and will hold in confidence all personal matters committed to my keeping and all family affairs coming to my knowledge in the practice of my calling. With loyalty will I endeavor to aid the physician in his work, and devote myself to the welfare of those committed to my care.[1]

Florence Nightingale (1820–1910) was an English social reformer and statistician as well as the founder of modern nursing. Her most significant contribution to humanity was when she volunteered to help tend to soldiers' wounds in the Crimean War. Later in life, Florence tried to bring reforms that addressed the hygiene problems of

---

1. "Nightingale Pledge," *Wikipedia, The Free Encyclopedia,* https://en.wikipedia.org/w/index.php?title=Nightingale_Pledge&oldid=1108182411 (accessed April 18, 2024).

the army hospitals. She was a leader who pointed the way for others, ran forward to scout the future, and advanced ahead of others to see what awaited them. In other words, Florence was a forerunner with the ability to live in the present while looking toward the future. And she knew how to lead by way of example.

We learn from Florence Nightingale that the one who *leads* can make a difference in everyone around them. A faithful leader stands at the forefront of a movement or a ministry—perhaps even at the head of an army. Good leaders are innovative and unafraid to implement new ideas, methods, structures, or programs. The person who *leads* should be motivated, courageous, goal-oriented, knowledgeable, creative, enthusiastic, wise, and faithful.

We read about the Good Shepherd's leadership in our lives in Psalm 23:2. In that verse, we read not only that He leads us, but we discover where He leads us: It's "beside still waters." *Still waters* may be translated as *the waters of rest*. And notice the Shepherd doesn't lead us to water, singular, but He takes us to waters, plural. We learn from the psalmist that we can have this rest only when we follow the Shepherd's leading. In choosing our paths, we will not find the still waters, but as we follow Him, taking His yoke upon us and learning of Him (He who is "gentle and lowly in heart"), we will "find rest" for our souls (Matthew 11:29–30).

Our society cannot come to rest because of the misleading and wayward guidance from leaders who are wounded and bitter. It has been said, "Misery loves company." Unfortunately, bringing up hate and division has become more acceptable than leading people in love and into healing. Forgiveness is being replaced by vengeance and payback. *Leaders in our society have lacked the ability to bring people to still waters because they have failed to lead people to the Great Shepherd.*

LEADING

The Good Shepherd wants to *lead*, but the sheep must follow. It gets very messy for the sheep when they don't respond to the voice of the Shepherd. Take Jonah, for an example. Jonah was the first Hebrew prophet called by God to preach the word of the Lord to Gentiles. He was sent to the city of Nineveh, the capital of the Assyrian Empire, which was an archenemy of Israel. He functioned in this prophetic calling around 820 BC, during the reign of Jeroboam II. Jonah's story is well known. After resisting the call (God's leading) to preach to Nineveh, Jonah found himself on a sinking ship and was cast overboard and into the belly of a great fish. In Jonah 2:1–9, we read:

> Then Jonah prayed to the LORD his God from the fish's belly. And he said: "I cried out to the LORD because of my affliction, and He answered me. Out of the belly of Sheol I cried, and You heard my voice. For You cast me into the deep, into the heart of the seas, and the floods surrounded me; all Your billows and Your waves passed over me. Then I said, 'I have been cast out of Your sight; yet I will look again toward Your holy temple.' ... Those who regard worthless idols forsake their own Mercy. But I will sacrifice to You with the voice of thanksgiving; I will pay what I have vowed. Salvation is of the LORD."

Jonah suffered the consequences of his unwillingness to be led by the Good Shepherd. Though called to prophesy to the people of Nineveh, he fled from the presence of the Lord and caught a ship to Tarshish. A terrible storm broke out against the vulnerable ship. Having exhausted all options, the ship's men reluctantly tossed Jonah overboard, hoping to calm the harsh winds and waves. Jonah should have stood before God on the people's behalf and then carried the message of repentance to Nineveh. Instead, Jonah ran away from his calling because he was offended by God. He was a reluctant undershepherd, but God used Jonah's calamity to force Jonah to become an obedient undershepherd. The men on the boat cried out, and God answered them by sending a fish that swallowed Jonah, and that fish caused Jonah to cry out. Jonah's cry in the fish set into motion the journey to Nineveh he had resisted.

The dependency the Lord desires His sheep to experience stems from the truth that we can do nothing apart from Him (see John 15:5). The Good Shepherd will lead people to the *still waters,* but the sheep must submit to the leading of His hand. And the leaders in our society must help people to know the true Shepherd who knows how and where to lead His sheep.

LISTENING

Most farmers believe healthy sheep drink up to four liters of water daily. They will voluntarily drink more water if the food they eat has more salt or protein or if their feed is dry. The beauty of *still waters* is that the sheep will drink from them without fear. The Good Shepherd leads His sheep to waters that are healthy and drinkable. When we listen to the Lord, we experience blessings, as we read in the following verses:

- "Come, you children, listen to me; I will teach you the fear of the Lord" (Psalm 34:11).

- "But whoever listens to me will dwell safely, and will be secure, without fear of evil" (Proverbs 7:24).

- "Now therefore, listen to me, my children, for blessed are those who keep my ways" (Proverbs 8:32).

A characteristic of the Good Shepherd is that He has a heart to listen to His sheep. The Shepherd attends and stands by them no matter what the cost. The Shepherd knows His sheep. He calls them by name! The sheep know Him; they know His voice (see John 10:14, 27). The Shepherd's heart is with His flock, not separate from them. The Shepherd knows His sheep personally, understanding their needs, concerns, and problems. The Shepherd's heart is willing to leave the ninety-nine in the fold and go into the darkness of the night to find the straying lamb that has wandered away from the safety of the flock and has been caught in the thicket of disillusionment and sin:

> "What do you think? If a man has a hundred sheep, and one of them goes astray, does he not leave the ninety-nine and go to the mountains to seek the one that is

straying? And if he should find it, assuredly, I say to you, he rejoices more over that sheep than over the ninety-nine that did not go astray."

MATTHEW 18:12–13

In 1 Peter, the apostle wrote to the churches scattered throughout Asia Minor, and he addressed the leaders as *shepherds*. Looking into his past and beyond these words of encouragement in his first letter, we can see the heart of Peter, who was once a tough-minded chief executive officer of a thriving fishing business. Then, he met and followed the leading of Jesus Christ, who taught him the ways of a caring and compassionate shepherd. Peter wrote:

> The elders who are among you I exhort, I who am a fellow elder and a witness of the sufferings of Christ, and also a partaker of the glory that will be revealed: Shepherd the flock of God which is among you, serving as overseers, not by compulsion

but willingly, not for dishonest gain but eagerly; nor as being lords over those entrusted to you, but being examples to the flock; and when the Chief Shepherd appears, you will receive the crown of glory that does not fade away.

1 PETER 5:1–4

We can only imagine the various stories that must have come to Peter's mind as he dictated this passage of Scripture on the qualities of a shepherd. He had heard Jesus deliver a piercing message to the Pharisees in Jerusalem after they had thrown the blind man, whom Jesus had healed, out of the synagogue. At that moment, Jesus had found him, and having opened his eyes physically, He gently and compassionately opened the eyes of his understanding (see John 9:34–39). And it's not an accident that Jesus next turned to the Pharisees, contrasting His ministry to this man with their harsh and sarcastic actions, and said He was the Good Shepherd who lays down His life for the sheep (see John 10:11–13).

The Pharisees considered themselves spiritual

leaders, but they were anything but shepherds. The way they had treated the poor beggar, as well as his family, demonstrated their ugly desire for power, prestige, and position. They acted more like devouring wolves because it was evident that they didn't care about the man's body or his soul. Jesus' words to the Pharisees about shepherding were also meant for Peter. As the Holy Spirit brought this story and Jesus' words to his mind, he would vividly and painfully remember his role as a "hired hand" who ran away rather than stayed as a true shepherd who would not abandon the sheep when the wolves attacked. Peter had publicly boasted that, if any of the other apostles forsook the Lord, he would not! And when Jesus predicted that Peter would deny Him three times, Peter argued that he would die with Christ before he would disown Him (see Luke 22:33–34). Though Peter did deny the Lord and fled just like the other disciples, he came to his senses, wept bitterly, and began his journey back as a humble servant.

Years later, as Peter addressed the overseers in churches throughout Asia Minor, the apostle did so from a position of great humility, calling himself a *fellow elder,* in essence, a fellow shepherd. Though he had been called and appointed by Jesus Christ to a leadership position in Christendom—the leader of the apostles—he addressed these men from an equal position. What a lesson this is for those of us who are involved in leading people in this broken society. Though we may have a definite leadership role, as did Peter, we are indeed "fellow shepherds" with those who serve with us!

Peter gave elders two exhortations as shepherds: Be *"eager to serve"* and avoid *"lording it over those entrusted to you."* His appeal to be *"eager to serve"* grew from another memory. It happened in the upper room when Jesus washed the disciples' feet. This encounter was another embarrassing moment for Peter. He had watched the Lord get up in the middle of the Passover meal and take the place of a servant, washing the feet of the disciples. Embarrassed, Peter resisted, primarily because he understood this was an oversight when he and John had arranged for this event. It was unheard of for the honored guest to perform this kind of servant's responsibility.

Again, as Peter addressed the overseers in his

letter, he could speak out of experience, having learned a lesson from Jesus, who was definitely *"eager to serve,"* even though He was their Lord and Teacher. *"I have set you an example,"* Jesus said, *"that you should do as I have done for you"* (John 13:15). Again, what a powerful lesson for all those who desire to be involved in leading. He that is greatest is to be a servant of all! Peter was passing that lesson on to his fellow elders—and all of us.

Peter certainly had another painful recollection regarding what happened during that same Passover meal with the apostles. Just before the time the Good Shepherd was ready to lay down His life for the sheep, it says, "Now there was also a dispute among them, as to which of them should be considered the greatest" (Luke 22:24). Though James and John may have precipitated this argument, Peter must have been involved as well. No doubt with sorrow in His eyes, Jesus addressed them with these words:

> The kings of the Gentiles exercise lordship over them, and those who exercise authority over them are called "benefactors."

> But not so among you; on the contrary, he who is greatest among you, let him be as the younger, and he who governs as he who serves. For who is greater, he who sits at the table, or he who serves? Is it not he who sits at the table? Yet I am among you as the One who serves.
>
> LUKE 22:25–27

Jesus had set the example of true servant-leadership. Again, Peter passed on the lesson he had learned personally not to be when he had said to the elders not to lord it over those who were in their trust (see 1 Peter 5:3).

Perhaps Peter's greatest shepherding lesson came early one morning on the seashore in Galilee. He had once again returned to what he did best as a professional fisherman; he went fishing. But he and several other apostles failed, having unsuccessfully fished all night. Once again, Jesus appeared and miraculously filled their nets. But the conversation on the seashore must have changed Peter's life forever. Jesus asked Peter if he loved Him three times, reminding him of that bitter experience before the cross when he had denied the Lord three times. However, the words that continued to impact his life were when Jesus charged him to be a shepherd to the other disciples. They were still *lambs* that needed to be fed (see John 21:15). Though they were in actuality supposed to be *sheep*, they needed special care and encouragement (see John 21:16–17). Jesus' prayer for Peter was now being fulfilled, that his faith would "not fail" and when he "turned back," to be able to "strengthen [his] brothers" (Luke 22:32) by being a "good shepherd" to those who needed to know the Good Shepherd.

When Jesus identified Himself as the Good Shepherd, He made a statement that Peter may have initially missed altogether—namely, that He had "other sheep" that were "not of this sheep pen." They, too, would listen to the voice of Jesus, for "there shall be one flock and one shepherd" (John 10:16).

If we are going to understand the heart of the Shepherd to heal people in our broken society, we must see that Jesus wants us to open the door of our hearts. He says to us today, "Behold, I stand at the door and knock. If anyone hears My voice and opens the door, I will come into him and dine with him, and he with Me" (Revelation 3:20). When we listen for the knock, and Jesus enters, we can be assured He will lead us by still waters.

LOVING & KIND

One morning while writing this book, my daughter was home from college and asked me what I thought about the apostle Paul. First, let me say that anytime one of my children wants to talk about the Scriptures, it brings great joy to my heart. However, my daughter was beginning to see the apostle Paul as having been very hard and authoritative in his teaching. Of course, her conclusion was unfortunate, but I understood that she was only beginning to go deeper in her understanding of the Scriptures. So, I endeavored to paint a better picture for her of the heart of the apostle Paul, and that led me to pointing my daughter to Paul's letter to the Corinthians, where the apostle dealt with ten different problems in the church. I didn't want her to miss the way Paul began his letter to the

Corinthians as he described their position in Christ:

> To the church of God which is at Corinth, to those who are sanctified in Christ Jesus, called to be saints, with all who in every place call on the name of Jesus Christ our Lord, both theirs and ours: Grace to you and peace from God our Father and the Lord Jesus Christ. I thank my God always concerning you for the grace of God which was given to you by Christ Jesus.
>
> 1 CORINTHIANS 1:2–4

The beautiful fact that the apostle Paul started the letter with kindness and focused on the church's position in Christ reveals so much of the Shepherd's heart. Another lesson gained is to see how the first ten verses in this letter all have the name of Jesus Christ as the focus. In other words, the apostle Paul wanted the church to know the Answer to her problems.

Most scholars will agree that the apostle Paul was the most significant pioneer missionary, scholar, teacher, evangelist, and hero of the Faith. Yet this early church leader knew that all his brilliance, multi-giftedness, and sacrificial dedication meant nothing if he were not baptized in God's love. No other New Testament writer spoke more about love or provided more practical leadership examples of love than the apostle Paul. Through the lifetime ministry and letters of Paul, God gave His Church, and all its leaders and teachers, a model of loving leadership. In all of Scripture, nowhere is it more clearly stated that love is the key to a broken society than in 1 Corinthians 13.

The love Paul speaks of is primarily love for fellow believers. This love was defined by Jesus Christ when He gave a new commandment to all His disciples to love one another "just as" He had loved them (see John 13:34–35). This love is expressed in total self-sacrifice for the good of others. Jesus exemplified this love by not only humbly washing the disciples' feet, but most importantly, selflessly sacrificing His life on the cross for others. John put it this way, "By this we know love, that He laid down His life for us, and we ought to lay down our lives for the brothers [and sisters]" (1 John 3:16).

Paul's first two descriptions of love in 1 Corinthians 13:4 are paired together and balance each other perfectly: "Love suffers long," and love shows kindness. You can no more have love without kindness than you can have summer without the sun. Scripture teaches that all those who lead in pastoral care are servants who must be kind to everyone (see 2 Timothy 2:24). "As servants of God," Paul wrote, "we commend ourselves in every way" by patience and kindness (2 Corinthians 6:4, 6). Like the Chief Shepherd, loving undershepherds are to be kind, even to sheep who criticize, reject, or oppose them.

A leader in our society without kindness is a disaster. For example, the Old Testament account of King Rehoboam, Solomon's son, illustrates how unkindness ruined his leadership. Before Rehoboam was coronated, the people of Israel came to him and demanded to know the spirit in which he would rule them because his father's rule ended in harsh oppression. Before answering the people, he rightly consulted with the elders, experienced men who had served his father and knew good and bad leadership principles. They counseled Rehoboam to lead with a kindly disposition.

They said, "If you will be good [kind] to this people and please them and speak good words to them, then they will be your servants forever" (2 Chronicles 10:7).

Unfortunately, disregarding the wisdom and experience of these older men, Rehoboam rejected their counsel. He foolishly chose the counsel of his young and inexperienced friends to treat the people with a harsh and heavy hand (see 2 Chronicles 10:10–11). As a result, the nation was divided in civil war. The people wanted a kind king, not a harsh one. People are no different today. Kindness is a key to effective pastoral care. We must cultivate a loving and caring disposition to reach and influence our broken society for Jesus Christ. Acts of kindness impact people in significant ways and capture their attention: a visit, a card sent to one who is sick, a concerned phone call, a caring voice, a thoughtful gesture, a simple expression of interest in another's concerns. The way of kindness is the "more excellent way" that can bring healing to broken lives.

Many famous paintings have pictured Jesus as the Good Shepherd, carrying a lamb over His shoulders or in His arms. Some of the earliest artistic depictions of Jesus found in the catacombs of Rome portray Him, not on a cross, but as a shepherd who showed kindness to His sheep. As we learn dependency on the Good Shepherd portrayed in such art, the One who leads us beside still waters, we will be used by Him to make a difference in someone else's life.

LET'S THINK ABOUT IT

God, though, wants to bring us into the place where there will be a dependence upon Him that no matter which way the wind blows and what other people say or think—or what the circumstance and environment might be—we will walk on with Him just the same.

IVAN Q. SPENCER

Group Discussion: HE LEADS

1. What stands out at you in the "Florence Nightingale Pledge" ?
2. How would you describe the way the Lord *leads*?
3. What is the significance of the *still waters*?

A COURAGEOUS PRAYER
HE LEADS ME

Father, You alone can lead me beside the still waters. Help me be faithful to lead others to Your provision, to hear Your voice, and to experience Your lovingkindness. I declare my commitment to servanthood and to serve Your purposes. I am asking, Lord, that everyone who sees Your blessings in my life will acknowledge You as the source so that they, too, would give You glory.

Write out your prayer today:

THREE
HE RESTORES ME

He restores my soul. . . .

PSALM 23:3

In 1964, my mother was eight months pregnant and was involved in a severe car accident. She was rushed to the local hospital by way of ambulance and was admitted for testing and observation. At that time, my mother already had three other children, a full-time job, and a very stressful pregnancy.

Eventually, the doctor released my mother after her more than one-week stay. The doctor told her to restrict her activities, and he expressed the need for rest until the delivery. But weeks later, my mother was back in the hospital to deliver her fourth child. The physician, Dr. Dennis, was very concerned about my mother's condition and decided it would be best to speed up the delivery by breaking her water and giving her a shot to help induce labor. My mother recalled the time right before the delivery when the doctor came to examine her and told her it was time. My mother's response to the doctor was that she was not ready. After hearing my mother's comment, the doctor slowly left the room and said, "Okay, MaryJane, let me know when you are ready."

My mother immediately cried and said, "Please don't leave!"

The doctor was only trying to help my mother find her courage and strength to endure. He stayed with my mother until she gave birth to me.

Immediately after the delivery, Dr. Dennis shouted out to my mother, "MaryJane, you have a son; thank God he is healthy, the baby is fine, and now you will be able to rest."

My mother's example blesses me when I think of all a woman must endure to have a baby. However, the joy that comes about as a result of a healthy baby being born and the presence of a child in the arms of a new mother overshadows all of the pain and discomfort a mother goes through. This birthing experience of going through the pain of delivery only to then experience the great joy that comes with the birth of a healthy baby showcases the kind of restoration the Great Shepherd can bring to our lives.

I also remember when my wife, Mary, was about to give birth to our first child. Let me start by explaining that Mary was in the emergency room four or five times during her pregnancy because of dehydration. For many women, the first trimester is the most bothersome; however, for my wife, all three trimesters were very difficult as her morning sickness and vomiting continued throughout her pregnancy. I remember frequently speaking to our child in the womb, saying, "I hope someday you appreciate all that your mom is going through for you."

It was the morning of May 22, 1992, that Mary said it was time. I drove her to the hospital fast like an Indy 500 racer. Mary didn't care, though; she just wanted me to get to the hospital.

The emergency room people rushed her right into the birthing room. I will never forget the experience of watching my wife go through the challenge of giving birth, but immediately after giving birth, the sheer joy of the moment swallowed up all the complicated pregnancy and laborious birthing. All Mary had endured was suddenly gone, and she was made new by the joy of her newborn child. To me, it's simply a beautiful picture of restoration.

RESTORATION

There is a longing in our society for restoration. The problem is people need to learn how to find it. Many look for it in all the wrong places, yet we can read in Psalm 23:3 where to find it—in the Shepherd. He's the One who restores our souls.

In Hebrew, the word for *soul* means *one's life*, so His restoring our souls is referring to His provision for our physical redemption and healing. The Great Shepherd is the constant restorer of our lives, of our bodies and souls. Restoring our souls may refer to His restoring mercy when we go astray or stumble along the way. We frequently need our Shepherd's tender and restoring mercy. We need the Shepherd to gently restore and heal us when we are lost. He brings us straying sheep back as we see in Psalm 60:1 and Isaiah 49:5.

Additionally, the words "restores my soul" can also mean He brings me to repentance or conversion. In other words, He restores my soul to its original purity after it was filled with sin.

When we put it all together, we discover that restoration is an act of renewal, revival, or reestablishment. It's the return of something to a former, original, regular, or unimpaired condition. It may refer to a reconstruction or reproduction of an ancient building. It can also mean the restitution of something that was taken away or lost, even putting something or someone back into a former position or giving someone dignity.

In Deuteronomy 30:3–6, we read that as Israel would return to the Lord, God would bless her, have compassion on her people, and bring her back from captivity. The modern-day regathering of Israel is even more accurately fulfilling this promise than Israel's return from the Babylonian exile. Today, Israel is populated by Jews from virtually every country in the world. This gathering is lovely to witness, and God's promise still stands. God will restore Israel spiritually as the final aspect of the promise to regather her people. He promised to circumcise the hearts of her people. This commitment was repeated in the promises of the covenant in passages like Ezekiel 36:26–27:

> I will give you a new heart and put a new spirit within you; I will take the heart of stone out of your flesh and give you a heart of flesh. I will put My Spirit within you and cause you to walk in My statutes, and you will keep My judgments and do them.

Indeed, Paul promised that all Israel would be saved (see Romans 11:26). And Jesus said that He would not return until Israel had embraced Him as the Messiah: "For I say to you, you shall see Me no more till you say, 'Blessed is He who comes in the name of LORD!'" (Matthew 23:39). When Jesus came to earth, He identified with the culture that He came to reach. He learned the language and lived according to the lifestyle of the people He came to call. In other words, Jesus came with a mission. He didn't come to earth to stay. He came to perfect, establish, strengthen, and settle His Church (see 1 Peter 5:10). Then He returned to the place from where He was sent. In doing this, He provided an example of how to bring hope to a broken society. Luke 4:16–22 says,

> So He came to Nazareth, where He had been brought up. And as His custom was, He went into the synagogue on the Sabbath day, and stood up to read. And He was handed the book of the prophet Isaiah. And when He had opened the book, He found the place where it was written: "The Spirit of the LORD is upon Me, because He has anointed Me to preach the gospel to the poor; He has sent Me to heal the brokenhearted, to proclaim liberty to the captives and recovery of sight to the blind, to set at liberty those who are oppressed; to proclaim the acceptable year of the LORD." Then He closed the book, and gave it back to the attendant and sat down. And the eyes of all who were in the synagogue were fixed on Him. And He began to

say to them, "Today this Scripture is fulfilled in your hearing." So all bore witness to Him, and marveled at the gracious words which proceeded out of His mouth.

Jesus Christ was the ultimate fulfillment of what the prophet Isaiah spoke. His mission was to "heal the brokenhearted." We also learn from the psalmist who declared: "The LORD is near to those who have a broken heart and saves such as have a contrite spirit" (Psalm 34:18). We can conclude then that, if Jesus had a mission to be near and to heal the brokenhearted, so should we.

REMEMBRANCE

Around 1100 BC, a man lived in Ephraim, whose name was Elkanah, the son of Jeroham. He had two wives, Peninah, whose name meant *pearl,* and Hannah, whose name meant *gracious* or *favored*. We learn from the Scriptures that Hannah was barren, which was considered a sign of a curse back in her day. Peninah, on the other hand, was blessed with children, and she taunted Hannah unmercifully, knowing how desperately Hannah had wanted a child. The Bible describes how this antagonizing went on for years, and each year, Elkanah would go to Shiloh to worship at the tabernacle. However, during one of those pilgrimages, Hannah reached a critical place in her life. No longer able to endure the pain of rejection, disappointment, and the ridicule of Peninah, Hannah, in desperation, went to the tent of meeting to seek God for an answer. Here's the biblical account:

> So Hannah arose after they had finished eating and drinking in Shiloh. Now Eli the priest was sitting on the seat by the doorpost of the tabernacle of the LORD. And she was in bitterness of soul, and prayed to the LORD and wept in anguish. Then she made a vow and said, "O LORD of hosts, if You will indeed look on the affliction of Your maidservant and remember me, and not forget Your maidservant, but will give Your maidservant a male child, then I will give him to the LORD all the days of his life, and no razor shall come upon his head." And it happened, as she continued

praying before the LORD, that Eli watched her mouth. Now Hannah spoke in her heart; only her lips moved, but her voice was not heard. Therefore Eli thought she was drunk. So Eli said to her, "How long will you be drunk? Put your wine away from you!" But Hannah answered and said, "No, my lord, I am a woman of sorrowful spirit. I have drunk neither wine nor intoxicating drink, but have poured out my soul before the LORD. Do not consider your maidservant a wicked woman, for out of the abundance of my complaint and grief I have spoken until now." Then Eli answered and said, "Go in peace, and the God of Israel grant your petition which you have asked of Him." And she said, "Let your maidservant find favor in your sight." So the woman went her way and ate, and her face was no longer sad. Then they rose early in the morning and worshiped before the LORD, and returned and came to their house at Ramah. And Elkanah knew Hannah his wife, and the LORD remembered her. So it came to pass in the process of time that Hannah conceived and bore a son, and called his name Samuel, saying, "Because I have asked for him from the LORD."

1 SAMUEL 1:9–20

Hannah was driven to such a point of desperation that she made a solemn vow to God: If God remembered her and gave her a son, she would give that child back to serve the Lord all the days of his life. The Lord of hosts heard her cry, opened her womb, and blessed her with a son. She called him Samuel, which means "His name is *El*," or possibly "asked of God" or "heard of God" because he came forth in response to prayer. A man passionate for the truth, Samuel became one of the Old Testament's most revered prophets, judges, and faith heroes.

Prayerful Hannah had a far more significant impact on Israel in her day than anyone could have possibly recognized at the time. After God gave Hannah her long-awaited son, she authored a beautiful hymn of thanksgiving to God, considered one of the most magnificent prophetic poems in the Bible (see 1 Samuel 2:1–10). Certain parts resemble the outburst of praise from the Virgin Mary many centuries later (see Luke 1:46–55). In Hannah's song, she also became the first person in Scripture to call the coming promised Seed the "Messiah" (translated in 1 Samuel 2:10 as "His anointed," from the Hebrew *mashiach,* meaning "Messiah"). The story of Hannah's heart of prayer, her song of praise, and God's remembrance of her all witness to the power of restoration.

We can take great comfort today knowing that God remembers that we need mercy and restoration. As the psalmist cried out in Psalm 103:13–14, "As a father pities his children, so the LORD pities those who fear Him. For He knows our frame; He remembers that we are dust." The Great Shepherd knows our great need and remembers. In Ezekiel 34:12, we read these words: "As a shepherd seeks out his flock on the day he is among his scattered sheep, so will I seek out My sheep and deliver them from all the places where they were scattered on a cloudy and dark day."

REST

In Matthew 11:28–30, Jesus gave an invitation to come to Him and find rest. He said:

> Come to Me, all you who labor and are heavy laden, and I will give you rest. Take My yoke upon you and learn from Me, for I am gentle and lowly in heart, and you will find rest for your souls. For My yoke is easy and My burden light.

His invitation is for us today. He calls us to rest, to take up His burden, which is light, and be yoked to Him.

This reminds of a story that took place in New Zealand in 2004. There was a Merino sheep named Shrek, and he became quite famous for eluding the annual shearing roundups.[1] Apparently, from 1997 until 2004, Shrek hid in South Island caves to avoid his wool being shorn.

---

1. Sarah V. Schweig, "Sheep Decides To Keep Wool, Hides Out In Cave For 6 Years," *The Dodo,* August 27, 2015, https://www.thedodo.com/wooly-sheep-hides-in-cave-1315578823.html/.

Shrek's owner, John Perriam, did not even seem to miss him for several years. After all, Perriam had 17,000 Merino sheep on his ranch. His Merino sheep were known for their prize wool, some of the softest in the world. Of course, Shrek's fleece continued to grow during his years of evading his annual shearing. Most sheep have a fleece weighing about ten pounds that's shaved (shorn) each year. When Shrek was finally found, his fleece weighed sixty pounds. That's enough wool to make 20 men's suits! Shrek carried this extraordinary burden year after year, and it continued to grow—all because he had wandered away from his shepherd. However, once he returned to John Perriam, Shrek was shorn, and his burdens were lifted.

Jesus, the Good Shepherd, is the One who can lift our heavy burdens. It is He who can shave our fleece and take away our self-imposed burdens. If you have wandered away from the Good Shepherd and life isn't what you want it to be, all you need to do is come to Him. There, you will find rest for your soul. Jesus' words of Matthew 11:29 echo the Hebrew text of Jeremiah 6:16—"Thus says the LORD: 'Stand in the ways and see, and ask for the old paths, where the good way is, and walk in it; then you will find rest for your souls.'" If you are looking for rest, you are promised to find it if you walk in "the old paths." This reward of rest can't be matched by anything our world has to offer. Restoration comes to a broken society through the loving actions of the Good Shepherd to bring us to His rest, but first we must accept His invitation to come to Him and to follow the ancient paths.

LET'S THINK ABOUT IT

Those who have not learned to find their satisfaction in the Father's acceptance always end up looking for it in all the wrong places.... The only place of everlasting acceptance is in the arms of your loving Savior!

BOB SORGE

Group Discussion: HE RESTORES

1. What do you believe is God's plan for restoration?

2. What is the significance of remembrance and rest?
3. Thinking about your need for restoration, where do you believe God wants to take you?

A COURAGEOUS PRAYER
HE RESTORES ME

Father, I thank You for restoring my soul. Today, I take time to remember all that You have done for me. I enter the rest You have prepared for me as the Shepherd and Overseer of my soul. I give myself to service. Freely I have received, freely I will give back. In Jesus' name, Amen!

Write out your prayer today:

FOUR
HE GUIDES ME

He guides me in the paths of righteousness for His name's sake.

PSALM 23:3

I still remember the day a sister came to my wife, Mary, and me for counsel about the condition of her marriage. For over 30 minutes, we listened to a wife who was passionate about how bad her husband was and how she believed he would never change. The husband was neither verbally nor physically abusive. Neither was he absent from the home. However, she was determined to prove that her situation was unique and without hope.

After she stopped speaking, she eagerly awaited my response, thinking I would see her situation as one that was dire and hopeless. I slowly began to talk, "I know what we should do."

"What?" She replied.

"We … we … should kill him!" I said

"*What?!*" she exclaimed, shocked by my "pastoral counsel."

Very calmly, I said, "Yes, based on what you have already said and how you have expressed no hope in your heart, we should just go ahead and kill him."

"But wait, that's not what I mean," she replied, trying to get me to rethink what I had said.

She didn't know it at the time, but I really wasn't advocating that we physically kill her husband. I was hoping the "shock and awe" approach would help expose a bigger problem—she had believed a lie about her husband and her marriage. She thought both were hopeless. She had been deceived.

Now, I don't advocate the approach I took because some individuals can be so very upset they might take a pastor up on his or her offer. I knew who and what I was dealing with. I knew and was very thankful that this counseling situation turned around when this sister, this wife, could see she had believed a lie from the same cunning serpent who deceived Eve in Genesis 3. And she had been only repeating that lie when she sat down to speak with Mary and me. Unbeknown to the woman, she was allowing the enemy to guide her.

We need to take a critical look at our speech. What we say, as Jesus told us in Matthew 12:34, shows us what is abundantly in our hearts. Those without God end up being careless with their speech. It is common for the unrepentant to speak lies, quarrel, gossip, repeat a confidence, talk negatively, complain, boast, curse, and find fault. They're following the guidance of the adversary and their own impulses. We should be different as children of God. And that difference should show in part in our speech. As the book of Proverbs tells us, there is power in our words: "Death and life are in the power of the tongue, and those who love it and indulge it will eat its fruit and bear the consequences of their words" (Proverbs 18:21).

Again, those who have not yet acknowledged their guilt and need for help tend to act out in a hurtful and harmful way. Their actions reveal their thoughts and hearts. Stealing, fighting, killing, promiscuity, adultery, arrogance, and rudeness are the actions of those without the power of God working in their lives. You see, if we allow previous experiences, rejections, and past hurt to dictate our future, we will never experience the power of God's goodness and mercy. So, we must look critically at our actions. We must ask ourselves, do we represent Jesus in a way that others would know there is something different about us and that we possess traits that others would aspire to obtain? My concern for God's people is for us to see the danger of living a compromised life and guard from looking to others to be our standard or guide. There is only one proper standard: Jesus Christ, as revealed in the Word. If we compare ourselves with ourselves, we will have a substandard existence. Furthermore, our compromised lives affect ourselves, the Body of Christ, and the unrepentant lives around us. The Body of Christ is weakened and sickly because of our compromised living. And regarding the lost, we are supposed to be the salt (preservation) and light (the way) to the countless souls around us. Are you salty? Are you shining? How will the lost and hurting ever know what faith, hope, and love are without our lives being examples of what it's like to be guided by the Good Shepherd—being guided by Him "in the paths of righteousness for His name's sake"?

While I was a pastoring in Bloomfield, New York, at a church called New Hope Fellowship, I remember encountering God in a very convicting and meaningful way. During that time with Him, I was very much aware that, one day, I will stand before Him and give an account for the gift of faith, the gift of hope, and the gift of love. It was as if the Lord asked me that day, "What have you done with the faith, hope, and love I have given you?" I knew in that moment I needed to be more aware of and intentional about sharing the gifts He has given me in an impactful way.

The Good Shepherd comes to those who recognize their need to be guided. As sheep, we don't need to strive to know where the green pastures or still waters are; all we need to know is where the Good Shepherd is because He guides us into what we need. And once we experience the Shepherd's guidance, we can be used by Him to help others look to Him for the same.

We must show the lost sheep the way to the Good Shepherd. We must tell them that there is a remedy for a compromised life. It's called repentance. They must turn away from sin and turn to the Shepherd in humility of heart. There is a better way, and it's God's way. There's no remedy without repentance or without Him. The lost are dependent upon the Good Shepherd. They just don't know it yet, but only Jesus can bring them to faith, hope, and love—providing them with meaning and purpose for their lives.

FAITH

In Romans 12, the apostle Paul spoke about how we should exercise spiritual gifts in the Body of Christ. He also warned us about walking in humility, as excessive pride often arises from those who regard themselves as spiritually gifted. Paul did not tell us believers to find pleasure in humiliation or degradation. Instead, he simply encouraged us to see the truth about ourselves and live in light of it. In other words, it is impossible to be given over to pride when we see ourselves as we are. He said:

> For I say, through the grace given to me, to everyone who is among you, not to think of himself more highly than he ought to think, but to think soberly, as God has dealt to each one a measure of faith.
>
> ROMANS 12:3

This verse reminds us that we should see even our saving faith as a gift from God and that we have no basis for pride or a superior opinion of ourselves.

Faith is essential, but recognizing where that faith comes from is even more vital to comprehend what faith is. We read in Hebrews 11:6, "But without faith it is impossible to please Him." Faith, therefore, is required of anyone who seeks God. One must also "believe that He is, and that He is a rewarder of those who diligently seek Him" (Hebrews 11:6). In other words, we must believe God is there and will reveal Himself to the seeking heart.

Wherever God may lead us, if we do not know where we are going, at least we know with whom we are going. We sometimes do not see the road, but we know the Guide. We must walk in faith and His strength to break out of our comfort zone and go! If we belong to Jesus, our lives do not belong to ourselves. First Corinthians 6:20 reminds us: "For you were bought at a price; therefore glorify God in your body and in your spirit, which are God's." The apostle Paul then said in the next chapter:

> For he who is called in the Lord while a slave is the Lord's freedman. Likewise he who is called while free is Christ's slave. You were bought at a price; do not become slaves of men. Brethren, let each one remain with God in that state in which he was called.
>
> 1 CORINTHIANS 7:22–24

To act like your life is yours and you don't need His guidance will never work. In faith, you let go and follow where He guides you. Remember these crucial words from Hebrews 10:38: "Now the just shall live by faith; but if anyone draws back, My soul has no pleasure in him." It is, and will always be, the Great Shepherd who guides us in faith. This faith has excellent rewards as we see in the following verses:

- "But Jesus turned around, and when He saw her He said, 'Be of good cheer, daughter; your faith has made you well.' And the woman was made well from that hour" (Matthew 9:22).

- "Then he touched their eyes and said, 'According to your faith let it be done to you'" (Matthew 9:29).

- "So Jesus said to them, 'Because of your unbelief; for assuredly, I say to you, if you have faith as a mustard seed, you will say to this mountain, "Move from here to there," and it will move; and nothing will be impossible for you'" (Matthew 17:20).

- "'So God, who knows the heart, acknowledged them by giving them the Holy Spirit, just as He did to us, and made no distinction between us and them, purifying their hearts by faith'" (Acts 15:8–9).

- "For in the gospel the righteousness of God is revealed—a righteousness that is by faith from first to last, just as it is written: 'The righteous will live by faith'" (Romans 1:17).

HOPE

When I was twenty years old, I attended a Bible College in Lima, New York, called Elim Bible Institute. While attending there, I was engaged to a high school sweetheart that I had known since the sixth grade. One night, while sleeping, I dreamed that my fiancée walked up to me and handed me the engagement ring I had given her.

The dream was so vivid that I could not shake it when I woke in the morning, and I found myself recounting it to my roommate. The dream disturbed me so severely that I skipped class at my roommate's recommendation and called my fiancée to share the dream with her. To my shock and great disappointment, she became reticent on the phone after I told her the dream. My fiancée began to confess that she was visiting me on the weekend to tell me she couldn't marry me because she could not be a minister's wife. The news was so devastating that, after I hung up the phone, I fell to the ground, crying like a baby. My roommate, Joe Zaino, the one who encouraged me to call my fiancée and share the dream with her, actually skipped class with me. And after I had fallen to the ground, weeping unconsolably, he dragged me into the bathroom so people wouldn't see and hear my loud cry. Being the great friend that he was, he just prayed and let me cry it out.

After a little while, I was able to quiet down a bit and catch my breath. Joe then began to share with me the picture God brought to his mind. He said, "As I listened to you cry, I was reminded that, when you were born, you came into this world crying. I believe today is a birthing process in your life. It's a day of new beginnings if you'll trust God."

I will never forget those words that day because I was infused with hope! God rescued me from the despair, discouragement, and defeat I felt at the breakup of my relationship. Hope was made alive as God's Word soon came rolling into my heart: "For I know the thoughts that I think toward you, says the LORD, thoughts of peace and not of evil, to give you a future and a hope" (Jeremiah 29:11).

The book of Luke details one of the most compelling stories in the Scriptures about hope. I mentioned this story in chapter 1 about the two disciples walking down the lonely road to the village of Emmaus. Their talk and concern, if you'll recall, was about the crucified Jesus. I can only imagine how empty, discouraging, and despairing that journey to Emmaus was. I envision their conversation going something like this: "I can hardly believe it. He's gone!"

"What do we do now?"

"It's Peter's fault; he shouldn't have—"

The conversation would have paused when a stranger came up from behind, saying, "I'm sorry, but I couldn't help overhearing you. Who are you discussing?"

The two disciples didn't recognize Jesus because "their eyes were restrained" (Luke 24:16). Let's look at the scriptural account for the rest of the story:

> Then the one whose name was Cleopas answered and said to Him, "Are You the only stranger in Jerusalem, and have You not known the things which happened there in these days?" And He said to them, "What things?" So they said to Him, "The things concerning Jesus of Nazareth, who was a Prophet mighty in deed and word before God and all the people, and how the chief priests and our rulers delivered Him to be condemned to death, and crucified Him. But we were hoping that it was He who was going to redeem Israel. Indeed, besides all this, today is the third day since these things happened. Yes, and certain women of our company, who arrived at the

tomb early, astonished us. When they did not find His body, they came saying that they had also seen a vision of angels who said He was alive. And certain of those who were with us went to the tomb and found it just as the women had said; but Him they did not see." Then He said to them, "O foolish ones, and slow of heart to believe in all that the prophets have spoken! Ought not the Christ to have suffered these things and to enter into His glory?" And beginning at Moses and all the Prophets, He expounded to them in all the Scriptures the things concerning Himself. Then they drew near to the village where they were going, and He indicated that He would have gone farther. But they constrained Him, saying, "Abide with us, for it is toward evening, and the day is far spent." And He went in to stay with them. Now it came to pass, as He sat at the table with them, that He took bread, blessed and broke it, and gave it to them. Then their eyes were opened and they knew Him; and He vanished from their sight. And they said to one another, "Did not our heart burn within us while He talked with us on the road, and while He opened the Scriptures to us?" So they rose up that very hour and returned to Jerusalem, and found the eleven and those who were with them gathered together, saying, "The Lord is risen indeed, and has appeared to Simon!" And they told about the things that had happened on the road, and how He was known to them in the breaking of bread."

LUKE 24:18–35

Jesus confronted these two individuals because they were slow of heart to believe. In other words, Jesus told them that the problem with their belief was with their hearts and not their heads. We often think the main obstacles to faith are our minds or intellects, but the obstacles actually have to do with what we believe in our hearts. Hope for a broken society can only come as our hearts are healed by what Jesus did on the cross for us. As the prophet Isaiah declared: "Surely He has borne our griefs and carried our sorrows.... He was bruised for our iniquities; the chastisement for our peace was upon Him, and by His stripes we are healed" (Isaiah 53:4–5).

LOVE

During my first few years in ministry, I was privileged to live in a log cabin with one of the sweetest couples I had ever met. Robert (called Rev) and Ruby Smallman were retired ministers from the Methodist Church. One day, when I came home from work, I caught this 80-year-old couple in the kitchen hugging and kissing! I stood there amazed that this older couple still had this passion for each other in their later years. The experience was healing because I wasn't sure that love between a husband and wife could continue to grow through the later years of life. Rev and Ruby's love was a fresh reminder of what real love between husband and wife should look like. Their love was an overflow of the love they had received from our Heavenly Father. As I spent time with this precious couple, I witnessed their devotion to Christ. They were continuously speaking and singing about God's amazing love and forgiveness.

In a highly revealing passage of Scripture, the apostle Paul disclosed the single, driving, motivating force of his life, and it was love:

> For the love of Christ compels us, because we judge thus: that if One died for all, then all died; and He died for all, that those who live should live no longer for themselves, but for Him who died for them and rose again.
>
> 2 CORINTHIANS 5:14–15

It's important to note that Paul was not speaking about his love for Christ but about Christ's love for him. In other words, Paul never ceased to be amazed by Christ's love for sinners, as demonstrated by His death on the cross. Christ's love controlled his life. It is the reason for all that Paul did. Hymn writer Isaac Watts captured the apostle's understanding of this love in the lyrics to "When I Survey the Wondrous Cross." The hymn ends with the powerful line,

"Love so amazing, so divine, demands my soul, my life, my all."

Understanding Christ's love is essential for a broken society to receive hope and healing. Paul, in one of the most magnificent prayers in the Bible, prayed that God would empower all believers to grasp the vast, incomprehensible nature of the love of Christ:

> That Christ may dwell in your hearts through faith; that you, being rooted and grounded in love, may be able to comprehend with all the saints what is the width and length and depth and height—to know the love of Christ which passes knowledge; that you may be filled with all the fullness of God.
>
> EPHESIANS 3:17–19

Although it "passes knowledge," the love of Christ is something we are to grasp intellectually, experientially, personally, and intimately. The most crucial aspect of guidance is knowing that the Great Shepherd is always motivated by love.

Love motivates everything God says and does. For example, "God so loved" that He made a plan (John 3:16). He gave us His Son, thus demonstrating that giving is loving. In His shepherding, God gives all He has. He's a sacrificial giver, a life giver, a reward giver. God is the "Greatest Giver of All." People continue to be in desperate need of His guidance. Guidance that leads to a right standing of faith, hope, and love will come to a broken society through the loving actions of the Great Shepherd.

LET'S THINK ABOUT IT

Out of the fulness of that heart of love, then, will spring faith, a faith for the seeming impossible.

IVAN Q. SPENCER

Group Discussion: HE GUIDES

1. How would you describe faith?
2. When you think of hope, what comes to mind?
3. Describe your own need for love?

A COURAGEOUS PRAYER
HE GUIDES ME

Father, I thank You that You have not given me a spirit of fear but of power and of love and of a sound mind. I pray to be found faithful to walk in faith, hope, and love. In Jesus' name. Amen!

Write out your prayer today:

FIVE
HE IS WITH ME

Yea, though I walk through the valley of the shadow of death, I will fear no evil; for You are with me; Your rod and Your staff, they comfort me.

PSALM 23:4

In April of 2000, Mary and I experienced one of the most devastating losses of our lives. After having two children and two complicated pregnancies, Mary became pregnant five years later with our third child. I still remember how I approached her about having another child back then. Even though I realized I was asking her to make an incredible sacrifice, possibly having to endure another complicated pregnancy, I still pushed my desire on Mary for another child. It wasn't that she didn't desire more children; it was the reality that she would most likely face another complicated and dangerous pregnancy. Despite her concerns and fears, Mary followed my request and prayed for peace and protection.

You could only imagine my excitement when Mary became pregnant with our third child. And despite the first trimester being filled with sickness, as were the past two pregnancies, she maintained a good attitude and continued to look to our Heavenly Father for strength and peace.

During the fourth month, while Mary and I were leading worship at a conference in New York, she noticed she was not feeling sick throughout the day. At first, we took it as a sign that the next trimester would be different and that God had heard our prayer for a less complicated pregnancy. However, during the end of the conference, Mary noticed she was starting to bleed. We didn't panic at first but realized we should slow down and get counsel from my wife's doctor. After explaining her situation, the doctor immediately instructed Mary to visit the hospital.

Mary and I had ministered to many couples who had lost babies; however, never did we think we would experience such a loss. It was personally devastating to me because I had felt like I pressured Mary to have another baby. To make things even worse, the hospital doctor covering Mary's case announced that the baby was no longer alive and did so in a very insensitive way, simply describing the loss as something that's normal. For Mary and me, there was nothing ordinary about this painful experience. If it were not for the comfort of the Holy Spirit of God, this death would have spiraled us into a deep depression as we were battling the feelings associated with the isolation and pain of grief. But we discovered in the process that we were not alone. Not only did we have each other and could grieve together, but we had the God of all comfort, the Good Shepherd, navigating us through the valley of death. Because He was with us all the way, caring for and even carrying us at times, we felt valued, esteemed, and loved. And when we came out the other side of that valley, we never counseled a couple going through a loss in the same way. Able to personally identify with their pain and disappointment, we endeavored to walk with them along with the Good Shepherd, letting them know how loved and valued they and their baby are to Him.

VALUE

When the Good Shepherd reveals that He is with us, our value becomes apparent. We no longer struggle with our worth. We recognize we are sons and daughters of the Most High God. One of the tactics of the enemy of your soul is to devalue your person and position as a child of God. The devil wants you to struggle with your identity and value, causing you to struggle with comparison, envy, and jealousy. Such things can lead to feelings of rejection, bitterness, and even hatred, which in turn can lead to strife and murder.

Consider the ideology of Hamas, the terrorist organization, as an example of what happens when the adversary causes people to devalue one another. When Hamas slaughters infants in their cribs, rapes women in front of their husbands, and takes women and children captive back to Gaza, that isn't because of some outsized grievance or ongoing dispute. It's because Hamas doesn't value the lives of Jewish people. Hamas doesn't have value for all human life as the Scriptures teach us. Pretending that members of Hamas are simply freedom-loving people who seek material prosperity, quiet family lives, and tolerance for those who think differently isn't just wrong; it's catastrophically blind. Hamas is a tool of the devil to influence the hearts of men and women to devalue children of God.

It's important, therefore, for us to understand how much God loves us and how precious or valuable we are in His sight. If we are honest, we may sometimes feel worthless or useless. We may try to search for meaning in life or discover our purpose. We may sometimes ponder, "Why am I here?" or "What is my value?" Have you ever asked yourself, "Why am I important to God?" You are not alone if such questions have crossed your mind concerning your value or personal worth. However, the answer to our value is found in the heart of the Great Shepherd, and we can read the following Scriptures to discover just how precious we are to Him:

> Then God said, "Let Us make man in Our image, according to Our likeness; let them have dominion over the fish of the sea, over the birds of the air, and over the cattle, over all the earth and over every creeping thing that creeps on the earth." So God created man in His own image; in the image of God He created him; male and female He created them. Then God blessed them, and God said to them, "Be fruitful and multiply; fill the earth and subdue it; have dominion over the fish of the sea, over the birds of the air, and over every living thing that moves on the earth."
>
> GENESIS 1:26–28

> For You formed my inward parts; You covered me in my mother's womb. I will praise You, for I am fearfully and wonderfully made; marvelous are Your works, and

that my soul knows very well. My frame was not hidden from You, when I was made in secret, and skillfully wrought in the lowest parts of the earth. Your eyes saw my substance, being yet unformed. And in Your book they all were written, the days fashioned for me, when as yet there were none of them. How precious also are Your thoughts to me, O God! How great is the sum of them! If I should count them, they would be more in number than the sand; when I awake, I am still with You.

PSALM 139:13–18

"Before I formed you in the womb I knew you; before you were born I sanctified you; I ordained you a prophet to the nations."

JEREMIAH 1:5

Hope for our society is found in the knowledge of God's personal involvement in our creation and birth as well as in His daily presence in our lives. We can know that we must be of utmost importance to Him. He cared to know the intimate details about each of us even before we ever came into existence. You could even say He knows us better than we know ourselves, and that's saying a lot! God knows us intimately, and He values our existence.

VALLEY

God wants us to know our value, but He also wants us to know He is with us during difficult and troubling times. He not only wants to be known as the God of the mountains, but He also wants to be known as our Lord in the valleys. The following story in 1 Kings 20:23–29 that conveys this truth:

> Then the servants of the king of Syria said to him, "Their gods *are* gods of the hills. Therefore they were stronger than we; but if we fight against them in the plain, surely we will be stronger than they. So do this thing: Dismiss the kings, each from his position, and put captains in their places; and you shall muster an army like the army

that you have lost, horse for horse and chariot for chariot. Then we will fight against them in the plain; surely we will be stronger than they." And he listened to their voice and did so. So it was, in the spring of the year, that Ben-Hadad mustered the Syrians and went up to Aphek to fight against Israel. And the children of Israel were mustered and given provisions, and they went against them. Now the children of Israel encamped before them like two little flocks of goats, while the Syrians filled the countryside. Then a man of God came and spoke to the king of Israel, and said, "Thus says the LORD: 'Because the Syrians have said, "The LORD *is* God of the hills, but He *is* not God of the valleys," therefore I will deliver all this great multitude into your hand, and you shall know that I *am* the LORD.'"And they encamped opposite each other for seven days. So it was that on the seventh day the battle was joined; and the children of Israel killed one hundred thousand foot soldiers *of* the Syrians in one day.

Many today believe God is a God of the mountains but not the valleys, and they tend to think God is a God of the past but not the present. They believe God is a God of a few particular favorites but not of all His people. Notice in 1 Kings 20 that God took the Syrians' thinking as a personal insult. These flawed and wrong ideas about God always take away from His glory and power, never add to them. Notice how God moved in extraordinary ways to defeat the Syrians, who had defamed His character in their flawed understanding of Him.

The valley suggests being hedged in and surrounded, but the valley can speak of some dark and fearful experiences. In Psalm 23, David spoke of "the valley of the shadow of death" itself but not death itself. It is a valley of the shadow of death, facing what seemed to David as the ultimate defeat and evil. David recognized that he may walk through the valley of the shadow of death under the Shepherd's leading. However, it isn't his destination or dwelling place. David understood that only one person can walk with us through death's dark valley and bring us safely to the other side—it's the God of Creation, the Giver of life, our Good Shepherd. Knowing God is with us keeps us from the fear that can torment us. Knowing the Shepherd walks with us enables us to experience victory.

VICTORY

As the Good Shepherd, Jesus repeatedly warned His flock about the deadly influence of false teachers. Many people, including Jesus' disciples, thought the Pharisees and scribes were true Torah (law) teachers and humble men of God. But they were not. They were hungry wolves who devoured people. In their religious zeal, they went far beyond the Old Testament rules and law by instituting thousands of ceremonial rituals and artificial traditions that made life almost unbearable for the people. They exalted themselves and were filled with self-righteousness. Worst of all, they hindered people from really knowing and loving God.

So Jesus sternly warned His disciples: "Beware of false prophets, who come to you in sheep's clothing but inwardly are ravenous wolves. You will recognize them by their fruits" (Matthew

7:15–16). With perfect moral indignation, Jesus identified their false doctrines and pride, publicly exposing them for who they were. This is what Jesus said to or about them:

- But woe to you, scribes and Pharisees, hypocrites! For you shut the kingdom of heaven against men (Matthew 23:13).

- Woe to you, blind guides… (Matthew 23:16).

- So you also outwardly appear righteous to others, but within you are full of hypocrisy and lawlessness (Matthew 23:28).

- You serpents, you brood of vipers, how are you to escape being sentenced to hell? (Matthew 23:33).

- You have a fine way of rejecting the commandment of God in order to establish your own tradition … thus making void the word of God by your tradition (Mark 7:9, 13).

- Beware of the scribes ... who devour widows' houses and for a pretense make long prayers (Luke 20:46–47).

Jesus' bold, thundering words against the Pharisees and scribes don't sound very loving and tolerant, and some people cannot imagine Jesus displaying moral indignation or expressing strong condemnation. But that is because they misunderstand who Jesus Christ is. His exposure of the Pharisees and scribes was the expression of God's just and righteous judgment on them. The God of the Bible is not only a God of love, but He is also a God of holy wrath and judgment. Divine love can be both tender and severe (see Romans 11:22).

Jesus is not an unkind, uncaring, and angry Prophet. He weeps before He whips. He cried over Jerusalem's rejection of His tender invitation to come to Him for salvation (see Matthew 23:37; Luke 19:41). He grieved over the hardened unbelief of the people and their leaders. Jesus is God's true Prophet and Teacher who risked His life to warn of danger. He is the Watchman on the city wall, crying out to protect the city from invaders. He is the courageous Protector who drives off the wolf, the lion, and the bear, for He loves His sheep. Jesus declared, "I am the good shepherd. The good shepherd lays down his life for the sheep" (John 10:11).

Our Great Shepherd wants us to know He is with us. In Luke 4:16–22, Jesus spoke in the synagogue of Nazareth, His hometown. He opened up the scroll to Isaiah 61 and read from the beginning of the chapter through the first line of verse 2. When Jesus sat down, He said, "Today, this Scripture is fulfilled in your hearing." Jesus is the person described in Isaiah 61:1–2, and He is the One upon whom was and is the Spirit of the Lord God. He is the One who is with us to preach good news, heal the brokenhearted, proclaim liberty to the captives, set people free from prison, proclaim the acceptable year of the Lord, and comfort all who mourn.

This anointing from the Good Shepherd is needed because there is a battle for the souls of men and women. The devil is unrelenting in his attack against God's people. We read in 1 Peter 5:8, "Be sober, be vigilant; because your adversary the devil walks about like a roaring lion, seeking whom he may devour." Peter encouraged us to remain clear-headed (sober) and watchful (vigilant) because the devil walks about *seeking whom he may devour*.

Some of the tools the devil will use are fear, deception, offense, compromise, and unbelief. He isn't just looking to lick or nibble on his prey; he wants to devour it—like the doe and animals in my dreams. The enemy can never be content until he sees people in our society destroyed. Do not, therefore, think that the primary purpose of Satan is to make us miserable. He is pleased with that, but that is not his ultimate end. The devil wants to see us defeated and devoured. The good news is this: "For this purpose, the Son of God was manifested, that He might destroy the works of the devil" (1 John 3:8). Not only did Jesus come to take away our sins as we read in 1 John 3:5, but in verse 8 of that chapter, we read that Jesus came to destroy the works of the devil! Jesus didn't come to just neutralize the devil's works. Jesus didn't come to alleviate or limit his works. No, Jesus came to obliterate the devil's works.

Many people are unnecessarily afraid of the devil, fearing what he could do against them. If they only knew that the devil is defeated as we walk with Jesus. No human effort can overcome the devil's schemes; it will take the Messiah, Jesus Christ (the anointed One), the Good Shepherd, to bring us to victory.

LET'S THINK ABOUT IT

Do I receive the kingdom, or do I take the kingdom? Do I settle and quiet my heart to receive what He wants to give, or do I rise up in confidence and take my kingdom inheritance by force? Jesus simply answers, "Yes." The Holy Spirit is the only one who can teach us how to walk this out.

BOB SORGE

Group Discussion: HE IS WITH ME

1. Share a lesson on value that you have learned.
2. What have the valleys in your life taught you?
3. Describe your own experience of victory with your Shepherd.

A COURAGEOUS PRAYER

Father, I thank You for placing value on my life. I acknowledge Your faithfulness that has led me through difficult seasons. Today, I choose to walk with You and experience the victories that You have won for me.

Write out your prayer today:

SIX
HE PREPARES ME

You prepare a table before me in the presence of my enemies. . . .

PSALM 23:5

While writing this book, Mary and I experienced a very difficult and painful season. It was a season we did not think we were prepared for. It was a season of sickness, anguish of heart, betrayal, loss, and a frontal attack from the enemy. But God, who is rich in mercy and great in power, might, and authority, was faithful to bring us through, causing us to overcome.

Here's the part of overcoming we don't like to think about: *We can only become overcomers if we have overcome something.* Simple, I know, but it's the part we don't like focusing on. It's not the good stuff we must overcome; it's the hard stuff. And if we are honest, sometimes we don't feel prepared for it.

Our difficult season began with our daughter and son-in-law going through an early stillbirth of their first child. They lost their son, whom they named Elliott. When you see your children broken, hurting, troubled, or sick, you would take it and bear it for them if you could. This experience is the walk we walked with our children in the spring/summer of 2021. The pain was raw and was very deep. The anguish was, at times, unbearable.

Before Thanksgiving of the same year, we learned of an extremely hurtful thing in our extended family and felt the situation's pain and anguish. What we experienced cut our hearts to the quick and took us through a unique fire that, because of others involved, we have not been able to share. We processed thoughts and feelings we never would have been able to handle on our own. But our faithful Shepherd walked us through it all to peace and forgiveness.

Not long after that, we learned that my mother was sick and tested positive for Covid. She passed in a week's time. Her funeral was at Thanksgiving. My brother was unable to attend our mother's funeral because he was in ICU fighting for his life in a battle with Covid. Within a month, he passed also. Our sorrow deepened as I was unable to officiate or attend my brother's funeral because I tested positive for Covid the day after Christmas 2021.

From the end of 2021 until February 14, 2022, I battled with what was diagnosed as Covid-induced asthma. A severe upper respiratory sickness ravaged my body. Coughing to the point of passing out because I couldn't get my breath along with sleepless nights, pain, and tightness in my chest continued night after night. Medications, treatments, and constant liquids were my routine, still with little sleep. I found out about a doctor and received the right treatment. With the help of this homeopathic treatment and the foundation of the continual prayers of the saints, God turned the page. My treatments prescribed by my doctor were needed less and less, the coughing subsided, and I was soon able to sleep each night.

The challenging season continued the day Mary and I went on our first outing together after recuperating from my illness. It was Valentine's Day, and the day was supposed to include a doctor's appointment, medication pick-up, and a stop at a thrift shop (we love thrifting). We didn't quite make it into the building to thrift because we were in a significant accident as we turned into a parking lot. Mary's side of the car took the brunt. We were struck so hard that the car spun in another direction and into a rock-hard snow bank, more like an ice bank. As they say, everything went black, and then the realization of the crisis awakened our senses. All the airbags deployed, and chemicals from the burst ones dripped and squirted out. Smoke filled the vehicle. The urgency to get out of the car moved us to action. We quickly surmised we were okay and started figuring out how to get out, hoping we would not get hit by oncoming traffic. We were stunned and dazed, yet we were soon out of the vehicle and able to check on the other car and its passenger. We all made it, no blood, no broken bones, only a burn on Mary's side from the burst airbag chemicals that had burned a hole through her winter coat and sweater. After the shock, I realized I had jammed my thumb when my hand hit the steering wheel.

When looking at our vehicle, we could see that from the right fender to the whole front of the car, there was nothing left. As a result of the accident, the vehicle was ripped, crushed, smashed, and broken; the whole front end was a gaping wrecked mess. All I could do was thank God! I could not stop myself; I said it over and over and over throughout the night. God had spared us. The Lord had spared our children and extended family the pain of the loss of parents and spared our congregation the pain of the loss of pastors. We were spared! A flatbed came and hauled our vehicle away, yet we were left standing! Aware that we had been under attack, we understood the enemy's goal was to sideline us, silence us, and even kill us if he could. Hallelujah! We escaped! The Good Shepherd kept and sustained us. He brought us the victory!

Were there times of panic? Yes. Were there times of pain? Yes. Were there times of fear? Yes. Were there times of discouragement? Yes. Was there sorrow? Yes. Was there grief? Yes. But the Lord never left us! He walked with us through it all.

When I was too sick to pray, Mary joined Jesus in praying for me. When fear gripped Mary's heart, I joined Jesus to pray for her. And when we could not utter words, but tears and groans were our prayers, God heard and responded with His love and sweet presence. There is victory in our hearts, victory in our bones, victory in our minds, and victory on our lips!

I want you to know that you will triumph. Jesus is coming back for an overcoming Church—for His prepared Bride. We are not defeated! We are not cast down. No, "we are but more than conquerors through Him who loved us" (Romans 8:37). Stand firm! Hold on to your faith in God. He will cause you to overcome and triumph. He is preparing a table before you in the presence of your enemies.

PREPARATION

The *table prepared* suggests foresight and care. It is also worth noting that the words, "You prepare a table before me," offer a personal connection with the Shepherd. In other words, the goodness and care indicated by the prepared table are set right in front of my enemies. Also, we can see how the Shepherd's care and concern don't eliminate the presence of our enemies. However, we're able to experience His goodness and provision while our enemies are there with us.

When I think about the preparation of the Lord, I immediately think of how love prepares a welcome. For example, with love, my wife and I prepared a room for each of our babies before they were born. With love, my wife and I prepare for our guests before they arrive. Jesus, the Good Shepherd, prepares a place for His people because He loves them and is confident of their arrival. Even now He is preparing a place for us, as He promised, "In My Father's house are many mansions; if it were not so, I would have told you. I go to prepare a place for you" (John 14:2). In this verse, we can see the heart of the Shepherd takes the initiative to go and plan. Again, Jesus prepares a place for His people because He loves us and and is expecting our arrival.

Luke 22:29–30 also reminds us what the Lord Jesus has prepared for those who follow Him: "'And I bestow upon you a kingdom, just as My Father bestowed one upon Me, that you may eat and drink at My table in My kingdom, and sit on thrones judging the twelve tribes of Israel.'" The heart of preparation reveals God's provision, protection, and, most of all, His presence. The answer to our society's brokenness comes from knowing God's plan and purpose—only those who make the Lord their Shepherd can experience peace because of His presence.

PRESENCE

There are three important characteristics of the presence of God that must be understood. The first is that it needs to be viewed as something good. Psalm 73:28 says, "But it is good for me to draw near to God; I have put my trust in the Lord God, That I may declare all Your works." Notice how the psalmist drew near because he saw the great benefit and value of the presence of God.

The second characteristic of the presence of God is that we cannot run away and hide from it. In Psalm 139:7–8 we read: "Where can I go from Your Spirit? Or where can I flee from Your presence? If I ascend into heaven, You are there; If I make my bed in hell, behold, You are there." Notice how the psalmist understood that he could not flee from the presence of God. The psalmist, by the inspiration of God, spoke of *God's Spirit* as an essential aspect of His being and *presence*. He considered the truth that God is present everywhere, and there is no corner or dimension of the universe hidden from Him. *Heaven isn't too high and hell isn't too low; God is everywhere.*

Lastly, the third characteristic of the presence of God leads us to experience the fullness of His joy. Psalm 16:11 says, "You will show me the path of life; in Your presence is fullness of joy; at Your right hand are pleasures forevermore." His presence can be enjoyed by us now and in eternity.

For Moses, coming out of the bondage of

Egypt, it wasn't enough to know that he and Israel would make it to the Promised Land. In his conviction, the Promised Land was nothing special without the very presence of the Lord. Moses, you could say, was obsessed with the presence of God. We read the following:

> Then Moses said to the Lord, "See, You say to me, 'Bring up this people.' But You have not let me know whom You will send with me. Yet You have said, 'I know you by name, and you have also found grace in My sight.' Now therefore, I pray, if I have found grace in Your sight, show me now Your way, that I may know You and that I may find grace in Your sight. And consider that this nation is Your people." And He said, "My Presence will go with you, and I will give you rest." Then he said to Him, "If Your Presence does not go with us, do not bring us up from here."
>
> EXODUS 33:12–15

God seemed to answer Moses' prayer, but

Moses did not rest. He continued to press God to affirm the promise of God's presence. This prayer shows how boldly Moses sought God's presence for his relationship and the nation's benefit.

The Great Shepherd reminds us that, without His presence, we lose faith. We will always find a desert awaiting us when we fail to esteem the Good Shepherd as our focus. The presence of the Good Shepherd keeps our lives from being dry, desolate, and wanting. The presence of the Lord is powerful.

POWER

The power of God is beyond description. Although a tornado, earthquake, tsunami, or hurricane displays the powerful forces of nature, none of these come close to the power that God possesses. Militaries around the world are competing to develop the most sophisticated and devastating bombs, but still, nothing man creates can compare to the power of God.

In the book of Daniel we find a powerful story of three men named Shadrach, Meshach, and Abed-Nego. These three Jewish men displayed a good understanding and appreciation of God's great power. These men stood firm when challenged to eat impure foods, and they saw God bless their obedience. Their conviction gave them the courage to follow the ways of God, when the stakes were very high. No matter how brave Shadrach, Meshach, and Abed-Nego were, facing the fury of King Nebuchadnezzar was still extremely intimidating. Despite the intense intimidation, the men stayed courageous in their confession of faith. These men experienced the power of God in the presence of a fiery furnace. Let's look at their story in Daniel 3:13–25.

> Then Nebuchadnezzar, in rage and fury, gave the command to bring Shadrach, Meshach, and Abed-Nego. So they brought these men before the king. Nebuchadnezzar spoke, saying to them, "Is it true, Shadrach, Meshach, and Abed-Nego, that you do not serve my gods or worship the gold image which I have set up? Now if you are ready at the time you hear the sound of the horn, flute, harp, lyre, and psaltery, in symphony with all kinds of mu-

sic, and you fall down and worship the image which I have made, good! But if you do not worship, you shall be cast immediately into the midst of a burning fiery furnace. And who is the god who will deliver you from my hands?" Shadrach, Meshach, and Abed-Nego answered and said to the king, "O Nebuchadnezzar, we have no need to answer you in this matter. If that is the case, our God whom we serve is able to deliver us from the burning fiery furnace, and He will deliver us from your hand, O king. But if not, let it be known to you, O king, that we do not serve your gods, nor will we worship the gold image which you have set up." Then Nebuchadnezzar was full of fury, and the expression on his face changed toward Shadrach, Meshach, and Abed-Nego. He spoke and commanded that they heat the furnace seven times more than it was usually heated. And he commanded certain mighty men of valor who were in his army to bind Shadrach, Meshach, and Abed-Nego, and cast them into the burning fiery furnace. Then these men were bound in their coats, their trousers, their turbans, and their other garments, and were cast into the midst of the burning fiery furnace. Therefore, because the king's command was urgent, and the furnace exceedingly hot, the flame of the fire killed those men who took up Shadrach, Meshach, and Abed-Nego. And these three men, Shadrach, Meshach, and Abed-Nego, fell down bound into the midst of the burning fiery furnace. Then King Nebuchadnezzar was astonished; and he rose in haste and spoke, saying to his counselors, "Did we not cast three men bound into the midst of the fire?" They answered and said to the king, "True, O king." "Look!" he answered, "I see four men loose, walking in the midst of the fire; and they are not hurt, and the form of the fourth is like the Son of God."

The Septuagint (Greek translation of the Old Testament) says in Daniel 3:24 that King Nebuchadnezzar heard the men singing praises while in the furnace. We can only imagine how satisfied the king must have been when he threw the three men to their supposed death and how shocked he must have been to hear those same men singing! Nebuchadnezzar was amazed by the power of God demonstrated in not allowing Shadrach, Meshach, and Abed-Nego to even be burned. Nebuchadnezzar then said:

> Blessed be the God of Shadrach, Meshach, and Abed-Nego, who sent His Angel and delivered His servants who trusted in Him, and they have frustrated the king's word, and yielded their bodies, that they should not serve nor worship any god except their own God! Therefore I make a decree that any people, nation, or language which speaks anything amiss against the God of Shadrach, Meshach, and Abed-Nego shall be cut in pieces, and their houses shall be made an ash heap; because there is no other God who can deliver like this.
>
> DANIEL 3:28–29

The trial these three Hebrew men faced had

no power over them because Shadrach, Meshach, and Abed-Nego thoroughly submitted to the power and will of God. This story is a beautiful picture of the Lord's power in preparing a table before us in the presence of our enemies.

LET'S THINK ABOUT IT

This man's greatest need—the ever-glorious, all-powerful, loving and perpetual presence of God.

IVAN Q. SPENCER

Group Discussion: HE PREPARES

1. When you think of God's preparation, what comes to mind?
2. When you think of God's presence, what comes to mind?

3. When you think of God's power, what comes to mind?

A COURAGEOUS PRAYER

Father, I thank You that my heart does not have to be troubled today because of my faith in Your promises. I believe You are preparing a place for me that, where You are, I may also be. I trust that whatever dwelling place You have prepared for me in heaven will be glorious, and I will never have to fear my enemies.

Write out your prayer today:

SEVEN
HE ANOINTS ME

You anoint my head with oil; my cup runs over.

PSALM 23:5

Mary and I remember the days leading up to taking our firstborn to the college of his choice. We awakened each day, asking ourselves if we had prepared him enough for the moment. Had we told him everything he needed to know? We were going to be 19 hours away by car. Had we given him the tools he needed to know what to do without our immediate help if he were in trouble? He didn't know a soul there, and neither did we. In our minds, there were no known resources that we knew we could confidently call upon for help. We also were concerned about whether his professors would recognize his potential or would leave his potential unchallenged. What if he knew no one would recognize him for who he is? We so believed that God wanted to develop his gifting and calling, but would the college recognize these also? We experienced a deep wrestling in our minds, which affected our sleep. We felt so many mixed feelings —happiness, pride, sadness, fear, hopefulness, and perplexity—all at the same time!

On the morning of the last day of his orientation, we were reading our daily devotions in our hotel room. We started our time in the book of Nehemiah. The words from the New Living Translation jumped off the page. This phrase was there numerous times throughout our reading for that day. The words, "the good hand of the Lord was upon him," leaped from the pages of the Bible. We began to cry, then sob, and our sobbing turned to laughter. In those moments, we had to repent and ask God to forgive us for overlooking the obvious solution to all our inner turmoil. The Word of God began to answer all our questions. God Himself was the One who knew our son with his gifting and calling. He was the very One who gave them to him. He was the One who had placed His favor on our son in the first place, and it was that same favor with God that was going to give him favor with man. Total strangers would show him favor because "the good hand of the Lord was upon him." Such joy flooded our souls at the revelation of this truth. That's why we laughed and cried at the same time. God had brought us to a place of confidence that enabled us to release our son to the good hands of the Lord. Silly as it is, letting your child go after being a steward of them for 18 years is a real struggle. But we had failed to understand all along that we were not just cutting the proverbial "apron strings." We were releasing him to *the good hands of the Lord.*

This truth of God's Word continues to be my strength, courage, and confidence for my son, who is now a married man with a God-fearing, God-loving wife and two adorable children. The favor and anointing of the Lord are also upon our grandchildren. We are confident that just as God's favor has caused blessings for our son, His favor will do the same for our grandchildren. The Lord will order all their days because of His marvelous favor and anointing that rests upon them. God is faithful to anoint with the Holy Spirit, with healing, and with hope.

HOLY SPIRIT

In the book of Exodus, we learn how the holy oil was made. This oil was used for anointing the priests and the articles pertaining to service. It was regarded as a sacred compound that could not be imitated nor used as normal perfuming oil. To "anoint" means to apply oil to a person or thing, a practice common in biblical days.

There were three types of anointing: ordinary, medical, and sacred. Ordinary anointing with scented oils was a standard hygiene procedure (see Ruth 3:3; Psalm 104:15; Proverbs 27:9). During mourning, the anointing process was discontinued (see 2 Samuel 14:2; Daniel 10:3; Matthew 6:17). The dead were prepared for burial by anointing (see Mark 14:8; 16:1). Guests were also anointed as a mark of respect and care (see Psalm 23:5; Luke 7:46). Medical anointing was customary for the sick and wounded (see Isaiah 1:6; Luke 10:34). Mark 6:13 and James 5:14 speak of the use of anointing oil by the disciples of Jesus.

Sacred anointing had as its purpose, the dedicating of things or persons to God. Jacob anointed the stone he had used for a pillow at Bethel (see Genesis 28:18). The tabernacle and its furniture were anointed (see Exodus 30:22–29). Prophets (see 1 Kings 19:16; 1 Chronicles 16:22), priests (see Exodus 28:41; 29:7), and kings (e.g., Saul—1 Samuel 9:16; 10:1; David—1 Samuel 16:1, 12, 13; 2 Samuel 2:7; Solomon—1 Kings 1:34; Jehu—1 Kings 19:16) were anointed, the oil symbolizing the Holy Spirit, and they were then set apart and empowered for a particular work in the service of God. *The Lord's anointed* was the common term for a theocratic king (see 1 Samuel 12:3; Lamentations 4:20).

Furthermore, the Messiah, from the Hebrew word *mashiach*, and Christ, from the Greek *Christos*, meaning "the anointed one." The word is twice used for the coming Redeemer in the Old

Testament (see Psalm 2:2; Daniel 9:25–26). Jesus was anointed with the Holy Spirit at His baptism (see John 1:32–33), marking Him as the Messiah of the Old Testament (see Luke 4:18, 21; Acts 9:22; 17:2, 3; 18:5, 28). Through union with Him, His disciples are anointed with the Holy Spirit, too (see 2 Corinthians 1:21; 1 John 2:20). Simply put, *the anointing of one's head with oil symbolizes the favor of the Lord that's upon the individual.*

Since oil was emblematic of the Holy Spirit, we see that the Holy Spirit is not poured out to enhance flesh, but to glorify Himself. This also reminds us that the Holy Spirit is never to be imitated. In other words, there is to be no place for encouraging a man-made imitation of the gifts or operations of the Holy Spirit. Charles Spurgeon referred to the Holy Spirit's anointing as "unction," and he said of it: "Unction is a thing which you cannot manufacture, and its counterfeits are worse than worthless."[1]

Jesus told Nicodemus that we are born again

---

1. Charles H. Spurgeon, *Lectures to my Students: A Selection from Addresses Delivered to the Students of the Pastors' College* (London: Passmore & Alabaster, 1875), 50.

by the Holy Spirit. "Truly, truly, I say to you," Jesus said in John 3:5, "unless one is born of water and the Spirit he cannot enter into the kingdom of God." Legitimate conversion is the most supernatural thing we will ever experience. When we put our faith and trust in Christ for salvation, it is the Spirit who opens our hearts and imparts spiritual life. He then indwells us, giving us the confidence that we are now children of God. None of us would be Christians today if it were not for the regenerating power of the Holy Spirit.

The Spirit has access to all the wisdom and knowledge of God. When we abide in Him, He leads us continually into truth, causing us to grow and mature spiritually. He is our Teacher, and those who depend on Him will know where to go and what to do because they are following His heavenly directions (see 1 John 2:27). Romans 8:14 tells us: "For all who are being led by the Spirit of God, these are sons of God." If you are a child of God, you have access to the guidance of the Holy Spirit. And He is the best Guide ever because He has all the information you need for the past, the present, and the future.

Those raising sheep know sheep can get their head caught in briers and die trying to get untangled. There are horrid little flies that like to torment sheep by laying eggs in their nostrils, which turn into worms and drive the sheep to beat their heads against a rock, sometimes to death. Their ears and eyes are also susceptible to tormenting insects. So the shepherd anoints their whole head with oil. Then there is peace. That oil forms a protective barrier against the evil that tries to destroy the sheep.

Do you have times of mental torment? Do worrisome thoughts invade your mind over and over? Do you beat your head against a wall, trying to stop them? Have you ever asked God to anoint your head with oil? He has an endless supply. His oil protects and makes it possible for you to fix your heart, mind, and eyes on Him today and always. There is peace in the valley. Our Good Shepherd anoints our head with oil today so that our cup overflows with blessings! He anoints us so we are healed and ready to serve.

HEALING

Have you ever thought about the various uses of oil? We can cook with it, preserve food with it, use it as a hair conditioner, or even turn it into soap. This same substance is a near-perfect food, providing a great source of vitamin E and good cholesterol, the kind we need to fight heart disease. Those who eat it most frequently, the people of the Mediterranean, have the lowest rate of heart disease on earth. Additionally, oil can be used as medicine and is said to have remarkable healing properties for things like sores, cuts, and rashes. It's good for soothing burns, too. You can grease your door hinges with oil on a piece of bread. For thousands of years, oil has been used for religious purposes, such as anointing the sick or newborn and consecrating ministers or anything else considered holy.

Olive oil, when put into a lamp, provides light. In the same way, David wrote in Psalm 119:130 that the entrance of God's Word brings light. Here are a couple of verses that link the anointing with this kind of illumination:

- "But you have an anointing from the Holy One, and you know all things. I have not written to you because you do not know the truth, but because you know it, and that no lie is of the truth" (1 John 2:20–21).

- "But the anointing which you have received from Him abides in you, and you do not need that anyone teach you; but as the same anointing teaches you concerning all things, and is true, and is not a lie, and just as it has taught you, you will abide in Him" (1 John 2:27).

The truth is we need an anointing from the Holy One because our enemies can cause great hurt and pain in our lives, both physically and mentally. It takes the anointing of Christ to bring about the healing that we need ultimately. It's no wonder James 5:14–15 says:

> Is anyone among you sick? Let him call for the elders of the church, and let them pray over him, anointing him with oil in the

name of the Lord. And the prayer of faith will save the sick, and the Lord will raise him up. And if he has committed sins, he will be forgiven.

James said that the church elders, as they pray, should anoint the sick person with oil in the name of the Lord. Oil was and is frequently used in the East as a cure for hazardous diseases; in Egypt, it is often utilized as a cure for the *plague*. Even in Europe, it has been successfully tried to cure *dropsy*. And "pure olive oil" is excellent for recent wounds and bruises. This *anointing with oil* has been interpreted as seeking the best medical attention possible for the afflicted (oil massages were considered medicinal) or as an emblem of the Holy Spirit's presence and power. *Anointing the sick with oil* is also mentioned in Mark 6:13. However, the reference to sins being *forgiven* adds to the idea that James is considering spiritual work and healing, not necessarily physical healing.

On a rugged hill called Calvary stood a grove of olive trees. Jesus often resorted there with His disciples to pray and rest. Amid this grove, the olive berries were crushed by the vinedresser, and the oil was extracted. It was called Gethsemane, which means olive press. It should not be surprising to learn that this was destined to become the very place where Jesus surrendered His will to the utmost degree, being put under so much pressure that the Bible says that blood squeezed out through His pores.

The book of Isaiah reminds us that the provision for healing is found in the suffering of Jesus: "But He was wounded for our transgressions, He was bruised for our iniquities; the chastisement for our peace was upon Him, and by His stripes, we are healed" (Isaiah 53:5).

There has been much debate as to whether Isaiah had in mind spiritual healing or physical healing. As this passage is quoted in the New Testament, we see more of the thought. In Matthew 8:16–17, the view is of physical healing. In 1 Peter 2:24–25, the view is of spiritual healing. We can safely say that God has both aspects of healing in view, and the suffering of Jesus provides for both our physical and spiritual healing. Without reservation, we can say that perfect, complete healing is God's promise to every believer in Jesus Christ, paid for by His stripes and the totality of His work for us. But we must also say that it is not promised to every believer *right now,* just as the totality of our salvation is not promised to us *right now.* The Bible states that we *have been saved,* that we are *being saved,* and that we *will be saved* (see 1 Corinthians 1:18; 3:15; Ephesians 2:8). Even so, there is a sense in which we *have been healed,* are *being healed,* and one day *will be healed.* God's ultimate healing is called "resurrection," and it is a glorious promise to every believer. The partial healing in this present age anticipates the ultimate healing that will come.

As we follow the Good Shepherd, we will find hope in the message and teachings of Jesus Christ and His power to transform lives and restore broken people. It is apparent in the Scriptures that Jesus provides a transformative power that can bring about healing at individual, community, and societal levels. Having a personal relationship with Jesus and living according to His teachings can lead to hope and redemptive changes in society.

HOPE

The Good Shepherd brings hope to our broken society in several ways. The first is that Jesus Christ offers salvation and forgiveness of sins. His teachings emphasize the importance of repentance and turning away from destructive behaviors. This message brings hope to individuals by providing them with a new beginning and the opportunity to live a meaningful and purposeful life.

Secondly, the Good Shepherd offers unconditional love and acceptance. Jesus' teaching about unconditional love and acceptance revolves around loving one another, even our enemies, and treating others respectfully and kindly. In a society where division, conflict, and discrimination exist, the message of love and acceptance from the Good Shepherd brings hope for healing, reconciliation, and unity.

Thirdly, the Scriptures teach us how the Good Shepherd demonstrated great compassion and empathy for the broken and contrite in heart. He actively helped the poor, healed the sick, and comforted the brokenhearted. The example of Christ's compassion brings hope to society by inspiring individuals to care for one another and uplift those who are suffering.

Next, the Good Shepherd's teachings offer a sense of purpose and meaning. Jesus Christ emphasizes values such as righteousness, justice, honesty, and integrity. By aligning one's life with these principles, individuals can find fulfillment and contribute positively to society. This sense of purpose brings hope by giving people a reason to excel in personal and collective growth.

Lastly, the Good Shepherd offers eternal hope. Jesus' promise of everlasting life gives believers hope beyond this earthly existence. He taught about the Kingdom of God and the hope of being in the presence of God forever. This promise provides comfort and assurance, especially in the face of suffering, loss, and uncertainty. Jesus Christ brings hope to society by offering salvation, love, compassion, purpose, and the assurance of eternal life. His guidance leads us to have a cup that runs over with a hope that does not disappoint: "Now hope does not disappoint because the love of God has been poured out in our hearts by the Holy Spirit who was given to us" (Romans 5:5).

Hope does not disappoint us because we think the right thoughts about God. For example, we meditate on how God's love has been poured out in our hearts. What does Proverbs 3:27 mean when it says, "As a man thinks in his heart, so he is"? What we think about, what we meditate on, impacts our perspective and attitude. If we think empty thoughts, that sort of thinking brings nothing of substance to our lives. It creates a vacuum of sorts, a vacuum of emptiness.

Furthermore, our thoughts have a progression. I've heard it quoted many times, "If you sow a thought, you will reap a deed; when you sow a deed, you reap a habit; when you sow a habit, you reap a lifestyle; and when you sow a lifestyle, you reap a destiny." Our thought life has the power to shape who we are and become as well as shape our eventual destiny. Are we doomed, then, if we struggle with negative or empty thoughts? Are we powerless to do anything about it? The answer is no. We've been instructed to determine who we become by choosing how we think. We can do something about our thoughts as we read:

> And now, dear brothers and sisters, one final thing. Fix your thoughts on what is true, and honorable, and right, and pure, and lovely, and admirable. Think about things that are excellent and worthy of praise.
>
> PHILIPPIANS 4:8 NLT

This scripture reminds us that we have the power to choose our thoughts. When I read all the descriptors of the things to think about—such as true, honorable, right, pure, lovely, admirable, excellent, and praiseworthy—I realize there is only One who is all of these, and His name is Jesus. Here is where I can use the Word to understand why these describe Him. In what instance was He true, pure, excellent, etc., or how about to me personally? Is there something worthy of praise for what He has done for me? When I meditate on these things, I am filling my mind with Him and His glory. And when I contemplate His Word, I can be changed to be made like Him. And when I am like Him, my destiny is sure! Who I become, what I will do with my life, and what is my destiny are wrapped up in my thoughts. So, let's fill our thoughts with Him. How do we do that?

First, read the Bible. As we read, we begin to see who He is and what He is like. We start to notice what He loves and what He hates. We begin to understand what is valuable to Him. We begin to feel what He feels. These thoughts and meditations are what form us, and we become like Him. So, we see how our thoughts determine who we become. We know that we have the power to choose what we think about, and we can be purposeful in what we decide to believe.

The Scripture also teaches us that we have tools, weapons as it were, to tear down those thoughts, reasonings, and philosophies that are in opposition to what the apostle Paul told the Philippians to think about. We read:

> The world is unprincipled. It's dog-eat-dog out there! The world doesn't fight fair. But we don't live or fight our battles that way —never have and never will. The tools of our trade aren't for marketing or manipulation, but they are for demolishing that en-

tire massively corrupt culture. We use our powerful God-tools for smashing warped philosophies, tearing down barriers erected against the truth of God, fitting every loose thought and emotion and impulse into the structure of life shaped by Christ. Our tools are ready at hand for clearing the ground of every obstruction and building lives of obedience into maturity.

2 CORINTHIANS 10:3–4 MSG

We can bring these thoughts to Jesus. These thoughts either measure up to Him and His standards (what is true, right, honorable, pure) or don't. If they don't, we can say these thoughts are taking us down a path that leads to wrong thoughts, lies, dishonor, and impurity. He will forgive us and cleanse us from all wrong thinking. Some thought patterns are so embedded in our minds that it takes a continual surrendering of these thoughts to be changed—and not only surrendering those unwanted thought patterns but then choosing lovely thoughts, pure and true, to replace the others. These new thoughts will bring about the likeness of Christ in us. They will determine choices, and those choices will bring about character, which defines a destiny. The Good Shepherd has a destiny filled with hope that will not disappoint.

LET'S THINK ABOUT IT

The anointing is imparted instantaneously when Christ smears our hearts with Himself, but it also progressively grows within us as we yield to Him.

PENN CLARK

Group Discussion: HE ANOINTS

1. What does the anointing of the Holy Spirit look like?
2. How does the anointing heal?
3. How is hope found in the anointing?

A COURAGEOUS PRAYER

Dear Lord, help me to understand Your anointing in a deeper and greater way. I acknowledge that the anointing grows as I embrace Christ in every trial, allowing Him to live His life through me. Anoint me for service in Jesus' name. Amen!

Write out your prayer today:

EIGHT
HE FOLLOWS ME

Surely goodness and mercy shall follow me all the days of my life; and I will dwell in the house of the LORD forever.

PSALM 23:6

In 1983, I received a small scholarship at a division one baseball college. As a teenager, I dreamed of playing baseball in the Major Leagues. Growing up in my small town in Upstate New York, sports gave me a sense of validation and appreciation. During high school, I experienced significant success on the baseball field, and my name frequently appeared on the sports page of our local newspaper. Seeing our names in print is a cherished feeling for every athlete. However, transitioning from a small town to a college in Staten Island, New York, was a significant adjustment. The challenge was even more pronounced as a freshman in college, trying to balance my baseball and academic commitments while adapting to a new social life.

Like many first-year students, I worked diligently to fit in with the popular crowd. Unfortunately, this often led me and others to follow individuals who were not the best role models in terms of moral values. I found myself gravitating toward a group that prioritized partying over being exceptional athletes and diligent students.

I remember that sometime during my third month at college I headed to lunch with some baseball team members. As I approached the cafeteria building, I noticed two men standing near the main doors, handing out items. Suddenly, it was as if I heard a voice within me saying, "You should be doing what they are doing." This inner voice startled me, making me even more curious as I neared the entrance. Close to the door, the two men distributed little green New Testament Bibles to everyone who entered. As usual, I glanced at my roommates and other baseball players to gauge their reactions. Surprisingly, I observed my teammates discarding the little Bibles into the garbage. However, having been raised by a faithful, God-loving mother who took her children to church every week, I felt deeply convinced that I shouldn't follow my teammates' lead this time. Therefore, I discreetly slipped the little green-covered New Testament into my back pocket and proceeded toward the food lines.

After lunch, I returned to my dorm, took that little green New Testament from my back pocket, and began reading some Bible chapters. It was as if I were returning home as I read such beautiful words of hope and purpose. I found out later that these two men handing out the Bibles were from Gideon International. (This organization is the same group that places Bibles in hotels.) Reading the Scriptures made me aware of God's presence in my dorm room. What was so shocking to me was that, though I was living such a sinful and self-centered lifestyle at the time, I was still aware of the presence of God while reading the green New Testament. This mercy and kindness brought me to my knees as I began to ask God for help and forgiveness. I felt like the Great Shepherd was following me into that dorm room and even around the campus.

I was reminded of Psalm 139:7–14, which says,

> Where can I go from Your Spirit? Or where can I flee from Your presence? If I ascend into heaven, You are there; if I make my bed in hell, behold, You are there. If I take the wings of the morning, and dwell in the uttermost parts of the sea, even there Your hand shall lead me, and Your right hand shall hold me. If I say, "Surely the darkness shall fall on me," even the night shall be light about me; indeed, the darkness shall not hide from You, but the night shines as the day; the darkness and the light are both alike to You. For You formed my inward parts; You covered me in my mother's womb. I will praise You, for I am fearfully and wonderfully made; marvelous

are Your works, and that my soul knows very well.

While reading the Scriptures, I was so thankful for God's goodness and mercy following me all the days of my life. Even when I was making bad decisions and living a promiscuous lifestyle, God was merciful and gracious. I can boldly say His kindness led me to repentance (see Romans 2:4).

It has been over 30 years of full-time ministry, and I can still remember this beautiful encounter with God at Wagner College on Staten Island. I will forever thank Gideon International Ministries for their boldness and courage in distributing Bibles on the college campus. The vision I received that day going to lunch has come about as I have shared God's Word with thousands worldwide. I am more convinced than ever that, when we make the Lord our Shepherd, we experience goodness and mercy following us. Most importantly, goodness and mercy follow us forever. Psalm 23 ends with the calmest assurance that the Good Shepherd will bring us into the presence of the Lord forever.

FOLLOW

The truth is that following the Lord as our Shepherd requires faith. Faith is essential in establishing a personal relationship with God and understanding His nature and character. Faith involves believing in something beyond what we can physically see and, sometimes, tangibly experience. The Lord is a spiritual being. Having faith enables us to trust in His existence, presence, and the truth of His promises, even if sometimes these cannot be fully perceived through our senses.

We know that the role of a shepherd is to lead, guide, and protect the sheep. Similarly, when we acknowledge the Lord as our Shepherd, we are entrusting our lives to His care and guidance. This requires trusting in His wisdom, sovereignty, and goodness even when circumstances may seem uncertain or challenging. *In other words, faith involves relinquishing our desire for complete control and submitting to God's will.* Following the Lord as our Shepherd requires acknowledging that His ways are higher and better than our own. It means yielding our own plans, desires, and agendas to

His divine purposes even when they may not align with our immediate expectations.

If you know anything about modern-day sheep, you understand that they depend entirely on their shepherd for provision, protection, and sustenance. Likewise, faith entails acknowledging our dependence on God and recognizing that He is the source of all we need. It includes trusting that He will provide for our physical, emotional, and spiritual needs according to His perfect timing and wisdom.

Faith is crucial in following the Lord as our Shepherd because it enables us to believe in the unseen, trust in His guidance, surrender control, depend on His provision, and walk by faith rather than sight. Through faith, we cultivate a deep and meaningful relationship with God, experiencing the abundance of His love, guidance, and care in our lives.

However, even with the knowledge and understanding that it takes faith to follow the Lord, we must remember that asking why during our journey with Him is normal. The Bible is filled with men and women asking God, "Why?" For example, consider the words of Job:

- "Why wasn't I born dead? Why didn't I die as I came from the womb? Why was I laid on my mother's lap? Why did she nurse me at her breast? Had I died at birth, I would now be at peace. I would be asleep and at rest" (Job 3:11–13 NLT).

- "Why do you turn away from me? Why do you treat me as your enemy?" (Job 13:24 NLT).

- "Why do the wicked prosper, growing older and powerful?" (Job 21:7 NLT).

As you can read, these are some very heavy why questions. Job was experiencing extreme physical pain as well as grief over the loss of his family and possessions. We can't fault him for wishing he were dead. Job's grief placed him at the crossroads of his faith, shattering many misconceptions about God (such as He makes you rich all the time, He always keeps you from trouble and pain, or He always protects your loved ones). In the Scriptures, we also learn how

Job was driven back to the basics of his faith in God. He had only two choices: (1) Job could curse God and give up, or (2) he could trust God and draw strength from the Shepherd's heart.

Now, let's take a look at why questions in the book of Psalms:

- "Why do you look the other way? Why do you ignore our suffering and oppression?" (Psalms 44:24 NLT).

- "O Lord, why do you reject me? Why do you turn your face from me?" (Psalms 88:14 NLT).

- "Let the nations say, 'Where is their God?'" (Psalms 115:2 NLT).

We need the background of Psalm 44 to help us understand the "why" of the psalmist. Israel had been defeated despite her faith and obedience to God (see Psalm 44:7, 18). The psalmist could not understand why God allowed this to happen, but he did not give up hope of discovering the answer (see vv. 17–22). Although he felt his suffering was underserved, he revealed the real reason: The psalmist suffered because he was "committed to the Lord." The apostle Paul quoted the psalmist's complaint to show that we must always be ready to face death for the cause of Christ (see Romans 8:36). Therefore, our suffering may not be a punishment but a battle scar that evidences our commitment and loyalty.

The psalmist's words suggest that he did not believe God had left him. God was still the Great Shepherd but seemed asleep, and the psalmist wondered why. In the New Testament, the disciples wondered why Jesus was sleeping when they needed his help during a storm (see Mark 4:35–41). In both cases, God was ready to shepherd His flock, but He wished to build faith in His sheep.

In Mark 16, even though Mary did not have the answer to her question, "Who will remove the stone?" she moved forward without knowing. She had faith in Jesus' leading. *Mary understood that His goodness covers every temporal need. His mercy fulfills every spiritual need.* Goodness includes every gift of His love and mercy, and every provision for our sinfulness. Not only will He love and care for us as His sheep, but His mercy will also guard us from the why questions the enemy of our souls wants to use to destroy us.

In the book of Job, more specifically Job 38–39 and 40:1–5, we see a pattern emerge where Job responded to his friends and then turned to God with questions and insights. This pattern changes dramatically in chapters 38 to 40.

After Elihu's speeches, God Himself spoke to Job from a whirlwind. In Job 38:1, God confronted Job, asking, "Who is this that questions My wisdom with such ignorant words?" God's response was a rebuttal and a comprehensive exposition of His creation and power. It's a stark reminder of the contrast between the finite understanding of humans and the infinite wisdom of God. The sarcastic remark in verse 21, "For you were born before it was all created, and you are so very experienced!" is particularly striking, highlighting Job's limited perspective compared to God's eternal presence.

God's dialogue encompassed the vastness of His creation, from the earth's systems to the stars and even the instincts and intuition of creatures. The example of the ostrich in Job 39, lacking in wisdom yet part of God's design, serves as a metaphor for the unexpected ways of the Creator. *This dialogue underscores the message that questioning God's wisdom is futile, as His knowledge and control extend far beyond human comprehension.*

In Job 40, God challenged Job directly, asking if he wished to continue asking questions. Job's reply was humble as he showed he recognized his limitations: "I am nothing. Could I ever find the answers? I will cover my mouth with my hand. I have said too much already. I have nothing more to say." This moment and experience with God produced a profound realization and surrender for Job. In other words, just like Job, it is not until we fully surrender and put our trust in following the Good Shepherd that we experience the favor of God in our lives.

FAVOR

In the parable of the lost sheep in Matthew 18, we read a story that demonstrates the favor and value God places on individual sheep. There were a hundred sheep in this story, but one went astray and was lost. As a result of one of the sheep being lost, the Shepherd left the ninety-nine and looked for the one who had gone astray. The parable shows the Shepherd's happiness when he found the lost sheep. He wasn't angry or complaining over his hard work or lost time. His joy in finding the lost sheep was overflowing.

This demonstration of the Shepherd is a clear picture of the favor and value God places on you and me. In the parable, Jesus emphasized the love and care we should have for all who have gone astray. In other words, we should favor what God favors and listen carefully to what is in His heart:

> "Take heed that you do not despise one of these little ones, for I say to you that in heaven their angels always see the face of My Father who is in heaven. For the Son of Man has come to save that which was lost."
>
> MATTHEW 18:10–11

The favor of God as seen through the Good Shepherd is an invaluable blessing that transcends human understanding. It encompasses the divine kindness, grace, and benevolence extended to His sheep. *Those sheep who experience the favor of God often find themselves surrounded by extraordinary opportunities, divine protection, and immeasurable blessings. God's favor is not contingent upon merit or personal qualifications, but is bestowed freely by His love and mercy.* It is a reflection of His unending goodness and limitless power. The favor of God can inspire hope, bring forth miracles, and open doors that seemed closed. It encourages and empowers His sheep to persevere in their faith journey, knowing that they are cherished and supported by an all-loving and all-knowing Shepherd. When the Lord is our Shepherd, we shall not want.

For those who are hurting in this broken society, it is essential to know that the favor of God can bring healing and restoration to even the most broken of circumstances. When life feels overwhelming, and pain seems insurmountable, understanding God's favor can provide relief and hope:

- It is crucial to recognize that God's favor does not indicate a life devoid of suffering or trials. Instead, it is the assurance that the Good Shepherd is present amid hardship and working behind the scenes for our ultimate good. His favor can manifest in various ways, whether through comfort, guidance, provision, or the strength to endure.

- It is vital to remember that even when situations seem despairing, God's favor can turn the tide in unexpected and miraculous ways.

- It is important to understand that God's favor is not earned but freely given. It is not based on our performance or external circumstances but on the Shepherd's unconditional love and grace.

Trusting in His unfailing favor provides reassurance that He is actively fighting on our behalf and working toward our redemption. The favor of God carries the power to transform our pain into purpose, our brokenness into wholeness, and our despair into a living hope. This living hope causes goodness and mercy to follow us all the days of our lives. Because of the Lord's goodness and mercy, we can experience fruitfulness in our lives. In other words, the Good Shepherd wants us to experience His goodness and mercy by allowing us to experience fruitfulness.

FRUITFULNESS

In December 2012, Mary and I arrived in the Cleveland, Ohio, area to begin a new ministry as pastors of the Christian Assembly in Richmond Heights. As our custom in ministry, Mondays were our days off at the church, so we decided to drive around the city and visit a new area each Monday. One of the days we were going around the city, we noticed small churches on every block for miles. I remember saying to Mary, "Why so many churches right next to each other? Can't these church families get along?"

Weeks later, we spoke with a native of Cleveland, and he explained the division or competition that was going on among the churches in the area. Our new friend also stated that these churches don't unite because of unforgiveness and selfish ambition. This comment from our new friend caused us to pray for forgiveness and unity in our city.

After Jesus' death, burial, resurrection, and ascension to heaven, the Bible says He sent the power of the Holy Spirit to His disciples on the Day of Pentecost. It is essential to point out that what took place on the Day of Pentecost resulted from intercession by the greatest Intercessor of all time, the Son of God Himself. Right before He collapsed in blood-sweating agony in the garden of Gethsemane, He uttered the most powerful and pivotal prayer ever to ascend to the Father of creation. It is found in John 17:1–26:

> Jesus spoke these words, lifted up His eyes to heaven, and said: "Father, the hour has come. Glorify Your Son, that Your Son also may glorify You, as You have given Him authority over all flesh, that He should give eternal life to as many as You have given Him. And this is eternal life, that they may know You, the only true God, and Jesus Christ whom You have sent. I have glori-

fied You on the earth. I have finished the work which You have given Me to do. And now, Oh Father, glorify Me together with Yourself, with the glory which I had with You before the world was. I have manifested Your name to the men whom You have given Me out of the world. They were Yours, You gave them to Me, and they have kept Your word. Now they have known that all things which You have given Me are from You. For I have given to them the words which You have given Me; and they have received them, and have known surely that I came forth from You; and they have believed that You sent Me. I pray for them. I do not pray for the world but for those whom You have given Me, for they are Yours. And all Mine are Yours, and Yours are Mine, and I am glorified in them. Now I am no longer in the world, but these are in the world, and I come to You. Holy Father, keep through Your name those whom You have given Me, that they may be one as We are. While I was with them in the world, I kept them in Your name.

Those whom You gave Me I have kept; and none of them is lost except the son of perdition, that the Scripture might be fulfilled. But now I come to You, and these things I speak in the world, that they may have My joy fulfilled in themselves. I have given them Your word; and the world has hated them because they are not of the world, just as I am not of the world. I do not pray that You should take them out of the world, but that You should keep them from the evil one. They are not of the world, just as I am not of the world. Sanctify them by Your truth. Your word is truth. As You sent Me into the world, I also have sent them into the world. And for their sakes I sanctify Myself, that they also may be sanctified by the truth. I do not pray for these alone, but also for those who will believe in Me through their word; that they all may be one, as You, Father, are in Me, and I in You; that they also may be one in Us, that the world may believe that You sent Me. And the glory which You gave Me I have given them, that they may be one just as We are one: I in them, and You in Me; that they may be made perfect in one, and that the world may know that You have sent Me, and have loved them as You have loved Me. Father, I desire that they also whom You gave Me may be with Me where I am, that they may behold My glory which You have given Me; for You loved Me before the foundation of the world. O righteous Father! The world has not known You, but I have known You; and these have known that You sent Me. And I have declared to them Your name, and will declare it, that the love with which You loved Me may be in them, and I in them."

Jesus prayed this prayer with His soon departure in mind. He realized that He would no longer remain in the world, but His disciples would. They, therefore, needed prayer to be kept by the power of God the Father. In other words, we need Jesus, our Intercessor, to pray for us (see Romans 8:34; Hebrews 7:25). The world, the flesh, and the devil are so persuasive, seductive, and destructive that we could never keep ourselves by our own effort. If we stay with the Good Shepherd, it is because Jesus has prayed for us: "Father, keep them."

The Father's keeping the disciples would not only keep them in Him, but it would also keep them united together. Jesus prayed that they would be one, and one after the pattern of the unity of God the Father and God the Son. The unity Jesus prayed for among His disciples has a pattern. Even as the Father and the Son are one yet not the same, we do not expect genuine Christian unity to mean uniformity or unity of structure. It will mean *unity of spirit, unity of heart, unity of purpose, and unity of destiny.*

Jesus prayed not only for the keeping and the unity of His disciples, but He also profoundly cared and prayed for joy to be fulfilled in their lives. His joy was the fruit of true faith and confidence in His Father. If Jesus was so concerned for joy among His disciples that He prayed for it, we know He is also concerned that we have joy. *God's purpose is to multiply joy in our lives, not subtract it.* The world, the flesh, and the devil would like to rob our joy, but God wants joy fulfilled in our lives. The joy of the Lord and the fulfillment of our joy have everything to do with being fruitful.

Matthew 7:16 says, "You will know them by their fruits. Do men gather grapes from thorn bushes or figs from thistles?" *In other words, fruit doesn't lie. It expresses the life of the vine.* That's why Scripture views the harvest in both positive and negative terms; it demonstrates the quality of our lives, whether good or bad. In other words, fruit cannot be faked. Though we may be able to feign a godly attribute for a brief season, in weak and tired moments, our lives will reveal our actual choices, priorities, and attachments.

Fruit also makes the invisible visible. It shatters all pretense and, over time, marks the true depth of our friendship with Jesus. We can't expect grace to cover up our neglect by producing spiritual fruit for us. Grace restores us to God's presence. *Grace forgives our sins and offers us a fresh start. But grace will not yield fruit when we have not paid the cost to remain in the Vine.* It will not make up for the times we gave in to the enemy's deception. Fruit doesn't lie. When it finally appears, it reveals what has been happening in the vineyard through all the seasons. And God's harvest is often full of surprises. The people we thought were pursuing God may not be genuine followers at all. The activities and pursuits in our lives may turn out to be fruitless or produce the joyful confirmation that we remained in the Vine.

In the time of harvest, only one thing matters, and it's our friendship with Jesus. And the depth of that friendship will be measured by the fruit we bear. The simple truth is that fruitfulness can only come when we abide in the Vine. Abiding in the Vine involves having a relationship with Jesus and being connected to what is in the very heart of God.

The sanctification Jesus prayed about in John 17 was about personal holiness and being set apart for God's service and mission. Jesus does not merely leave His disciples in the world but sends them into it to be fruitful so that we can say, "Surely goodness and mercy shall follow me all the days of my life, and I will dwell in the house of the LORD forever." Goodness and mercy are found in following the Good Shepherd. Jesus' prayer in John 17 reveals everything we need to remain in the Vine, despite living in a broken society.

LET'S THINK ABOUT IT

Where are those who are willing to risk their all and earnestly seek GOD with all their hearts? Where are those who are willing to walk in the light? They only will be rewarded with the greatest visitation that GOD ever gave to man.

IVAN Q. SPENCER

Group Discussion: GOODNESS AND MERCY

1. What keeps people from the goodness and mercy of the Shepherd?

2. What does "all of the days of my life" mean to you?
3. How do we "dwell in the house of the LORD forever"?

A COURAGEOUS PRAYER

Father, I recognize You today as the One who completes me. You are all-powerful. You grant me peace. I thank You and acknowledge You as the loving and caring Shepherd who has brought me into an everlasting covenant through Your blood shed on the cross. Thank You for my healing and deliverance.

Write out your prayer today:

CONCLUSION

Now may the God of peace who brought up our Lord Jesus from the dead, that great Shepherd of the sheep, through the blood of the everlasting covenant, make you complete in every good work to do His will, working in you what is well pleasing in His sight, through Jesus Christ.

HEBREWS 13:20–21

The passage I've concluded with contains a powerful blessing, calling on the God of peace to work in individuals and make them complete in every good work, thus aligning them with His will. This blessing mirrors the priestly blessing found in Numbers 6:22–27 that emphasized the attributes of God—His peace, power, loving care, and generosity:

- The Lord bless you and keep you.
- The Lord make His face shine upon you and be gracious to you.
- The Lord lift His countenance upon you and give you peace.

Our Great Shepherd is the One who makes us complete. We receive of His fullness, as John said, "grace for grace" (John 1:16). The blessings or graces expressed by God's very heart provide the hope needed for our broken society.

In a world filled with bitterness and destructive behavior, Hebrews 13:20–21 offers hope and points to the Source of healing. It presents the image of God as the Shepherd, who guides and cares for His people, and as the One who possesses the power to bring life even in the face of death. Through the blood of the everlasting covenant in Jesus Christ, believers have access to the transformative power of God.

The question is where people can find answers and hope for their brokenness. Peace can only be found in the Good Shepherd. The answer is turning to God, seeking His guidance, and allowing Him to work in our lives. He alone leads us to find wholeness, reconciliation, and purpose.

This blessing reminds us that there is a spiritual dimension to our existence, and seeking a relationship with God can bring healing, restoration, and a sense of purpose. It encourages us to trust God to transform our lives and work through us to bring about positive change in society. Ultimately, this scripture speaks to the power and hope of a divine relationship. It invites individuals to turn to God as the Source of fulfillment, purpose, and peace, highlighting His attributes and His ability to bring light and restoration to a broken world.

We must return to the Shepherd. He is the answer. In Him, will we find all that we need. As He said,

I am the good shepherd; and I know My sheep, and am known by My own. As the Father knows Me, even so I know the Father; and I lay down My life for the sheep. And other sheep I have which are not of this fold; them also I must bring, and they will hear My voice; and there will be one flock and one shepherd.

JOHN 10:14–16

APPENDIX
PASTORAL CARE

Shepherd the flock of God which is among you, serving as overseers, not by compulsion but willingly, not for dishonest gain but eagerly; nor as being lords over those entrusted to you, but being examples to the flock; and when the Chief Shepherd appears, you will receive the crown of glory that does not fade away.

1 PETER 5:2–4

It is a privilege to be used by God to encourage people, to help stand with and comfort those who face various trials. It is a holy calling! Each of us in our pastoral care has our specific work to do, and we must do it so that boldness may be ours on the day of the Master's appearance and so that no man can take our crown.

As the Lord always encourages us, we have that which can inspire others. We have Him living in our lives and revealing Himself through our loving, shepherding care. As servants of the Lord, we must come to Him with willing and surrendered hearts and ready minds, all yielded to the Spirit of the Lord. This means we must walk in humility and obedience to the Lord.

There are essential skills that pastoral care leaders can learn and steps that we can take to demonstrate to our church families the kind of leadership that Christ had for the Church when He loved her and gave Himself for her (see Ephesians 5:25). If you want to be an effective pastoral care leader, an effective shepherd, you must have these seven qualities or characteristics.

1. A GENUINE SPIRIT OF HUMILITY

There is no place for the pastoral care person who does not understand their desperate need for humility.

A shepherd must constantly remember that God is working with an individual who has "fallen short of the glory of God" (Romans 3:23). Past failures are a critical means of reminding ourselves that there is no room for pride. Every shepherd should maintain a "sanctified Hall of Shame" in the back of their minds. Whenever there is a tendency to be critical of a sheep, you should mentally revisit your "Hall of Shame." Remember, "God resists the proud, but gives grace to the humble" (James 4:6). Be a channel of grace as you minister to others.

God has the right kind of jealousy. He will not share His glory with another (see Isaiah 42:8). Whenever there is praise, the shepherd must acknowledge that God should receive the praise and that it is only by His grace that things are working together. The spirit of humility must carry over to those in the flock (congregation/community). A shepherd must emphasize the need for all sheep (members in the Body of Christ) to do what God has called them to do. The pastoral care person must also help the community realize their need for spiritual support and guidance.

A further aspect of humility must be demonstrated by the shepherd in admitting when they are wrong. If the sheep do not see the pastor or shepherd recognizing their weaknesses, the sheep will immediately interpret this as pride. They will also assume that the pastor does not need them.

2. EARN THE RIGHT TO BE HEARD

No shepherd should expect the right to be heard, and they should certainly not demand it. They must, however, earn this privilege by developing relationships with individuals in the community.

Relationships take time and are fragile. Any discipline a pastor administers to a sheep of their flock must be based on their relationship with that person. The basis of a pastor's commitment is to support each church member so that they are fruitful and to watch out for their safety.

When a shepherd earns the right to be heard, they must cherish that right and not abuse it.

3. RECOGNIZE THE VALUE OF EVERYONE

A shepherd must recognize each sheep's strengths and weaknesses. The shepherd must emphasize the strengths and see how they could provide training that would strengthen the weak areas.

A shepherd must commit to each sheep in the fold that they are dedicated to the sheep's success and God's reputation rather than their own reputation.

Sheep need to be reassured that their shepherd loves them and that, whether they are right or wrong, the shepherd *always* will love them. They can break the shepherd's heart by doing evil, but the sheep must sense that the shepherd will never condemn or disown them.

Although a shepherd must expect each sheep of their flock to fail at times, the shepherd should do all he can to help prevent it. If failure occurs, the shepherd should fortify the sheep to go through it in victory.

4. RECEIVE EACH PERSON AS THEY ARE

A shepherd must remember that every sheep has their rate of development. The shepherd must have a balanced approach in offering both supervision and freedom to fail. Too much freedom will be interpreted by the sheep as rejection. Too much supervision will be interpreted by the sheep as a lack of trust in them.

A shepherd must never forget how each sheep will need patience. They must also remember how far a sheep has come and be thankful to the Lord for the growth. A shepherd needs to appreciate the members of their flock for what they are now rather than what they might be in the future.

5. SACRIFICE FOR THOSE IN YOUR CARE

The very essence of faithfulness involves continual sacrifice for the sheep. It consists of yielding rights as Christ did. It is ensuring that each one in the flock is cared for before the shepherd meets their own needs.

A shepherd's sacrifice demonstrates to the

outside world that they care about their flock. The lack of sacrifice is clear evidence to others that a shepherd does not respect their sheep or recognize them as necessary.

A shepherd's lack of sacrifice will infect the flock. The sheep will also develop a disrespect for each other and put other sheep in harm's way.

6. BE DISCERNING

Discernment is having or showing good judgment or understanding. To be successful as a pastoral care person, you must have and use spiritual discernment based on the wisdom and knowledge of scriptural principles.

You must learn to discern the motives behind words, actions, and attitudes—not to condemn, but to help and protect.

For example, in 2 Corinthians 12:20, the apostle Paul listed eight sins of discord among the Corinthians that, if continued, would require discipline from him: "quarreling, jealousy, anger, hostility, slander, gossip, conceit, and disorder." This list of social sins is evidence of the "works of the flesh" that results in conflict and confusion in society. There would only be "want" and no hope for unity in the church at Corinth until there was an acknowledgment and repentance of these fleshly and un-Christlike actions. Pastoral care requires discernment and wisdom in dealing with these "works of the flesh."

7. DISPLAY THE FRUIT OF THE SPIRIT

God has always wanted those who are part of pastoral care to live in a way that would demonstrate His holy character to the unbelieving world. As people born of God's Spirit, each follower of Christ is a "new creation" in Christ (2 Corinthians 5:17). The shepherd must handle conflict radically differently from how it would be handled in our selfish world.

The difference between the old life before conversion and the new life after conversion is comparable to the difference between death and life or between living in light versus living in complete darkness. This new life is to be continued by faith in God's Word and dependence on the power and presence of the Holy Spirit. Nothing but the indwelling presence and power of the Holy Spirit is sufficient to enable followers of Christ to resist the desires of the flesh and to live a Christlike life.

The Holy Spirit seeks to form Christlike character qualities in the life of every sheep. These Christlike qualities promote right attitudes, godly conduct, and healthy relationships—the qualities our society desperately needs. The apostle Paul's list of the "the fruit of the Spirit" gives us a picture of Christlike character and conduct: "love, joy, peace, patience, kindness, goodness, faithfulness, gentleness, self-control" (Galatians 5:22–23). As pastoral care people, we know we are walking by the Spirit when we see "the fruit of the Spirit" demonstrated in our attitude and daily conduct.

The opposite is true, however. When pastoral care people act according to the flesh, they do not display the fruit of the Spirit. They have the potential to do terrible damage to the sheep and the name of Christ. "The fruit of the Spirit" should guide our attitudes and behavior when dealing with a broken society. So we should always ask ourselves: "Am I displaying Christlike character and the life of the Holy Spirit when I deal with brokenness and conflict?" Hopefully, pastoral care people will be able to answer: "Yes!"

REFERENCES
"LET'S THINK ABOUT IT" EPIGRAPHS

CHAPTER ONE

Frank Damazio, *The Vanguard Leader*, (By Bible Temple, 1994), 3.

CHAPTER TWO

Ivan Q. Spencer, *Faith Living the Crucified Life,* ed. Edie Mourey, (Big Flats, NY: Furrow Press, 2008), 2–3.

CHAPTER THREE

Bob Sorge, *Dealing with the Rejection & Praise of Man* (Grandview, MO: Oasis House, 2009), 24.

CHAPTER FOUR

Ivan Q. Spencer, *Faith Living the Crucified Life,* ed. Edie Mourey, (Big Flats, NY: Furrow Press, 2008), 43.

CHAPTER FIVE

Bob Sorge, *The Fire of Delayed Answers* (Grandview, MO: Oasis House, 2010), 177.

CHAPTER SIX

Ivan Q. Spencer, *Faith Living the Crucified Life,* ed. Edie Mourey, (Big Flats, NY: Furrow Press, 2008), 59.

CHAPTER SEVEN

Penn Clark, *Cultivating the Anointing: Discipleship House Study Notes* (Penn Yan, NY: Wordsmith, 2014), 5.

CHAPTER EIGHT

Ivan Q. Spencer, *Daily Seedings: A Devotional Classic for the Spirit-Filled Life,* sel. & ed. Edie Mourey, (Big Flats, NY: Furrow Press, 2008), 211.

ABOUT THE AUTHOR

Dr. Alan James Schrader is a former native of Upstate New York. He currently resides in Cleveland, Ohio. Married for over 32 years, he and his wife, Mary, have four children and three grandchildren. They presently have the joy of serving as Senior Pastors at Christian Assembly in Richmond Heights, Ohio.

Dr. Schrader is a graduate of the University of Biblical Studies and Seminary with a bachelor's degree in Theology. He went on to study at American Christian College and Seminary, where he earned an accredited Masters of Arts in Ministry degree. He then went to the Masters International

University of Divinity, where he earned a Doctor of Biblical Studies in Pastoral Ministry.

Dr. Schrader is the former President of IFCA Bible College and former Education Director for the International Fellowship of Christian Assemblies. He has authored several books and serves as a volunteer Police Chaplain for the Richmond Heights Police Department. He has a passion for effectively sharing the love of God with people every day.

Contact: Alan James Schrader Ministries– 25595 Chardon Road – Cleveland, OH 44143

Email: Drajschrader@gmail.com

Website: www.AlanJamesSchrader.com

ALSO BY DR. ALAN JAMES SCHRADER

The Book of Revelation: Bible Study

Songs & Psalms for the Community

Hymns & Scriptures for the Community

Practices in the Christian Faith

Practices in the Christian Faith: Teacher's Manual

Foundational Doctrines of Christ

Foundational Doctrines of Christ: Teacher's Manual

The 30-Day Devotional & Journal: Daily Walking and Talking with Your Creator

Words to Live By: Meditating and Memorizing the Word of God

180 Devotional Direction: Turn Your Eyes upon Jesus

180 Devotional Direction: From the Chaplain's Office

Financial Freedom: Teacher's Manual

BASICS: Christianity 101

An Introduction to the Old Testament Scriptures: Teacher's Manual

Introduction to Theology

Biblical Christianity vs. Other Religions

Winter Devotions: Part of the "Daily Devotion" Series (Seasons Book 1)

Spring Devotions: Part of the "Daily Devotion" Series (Seasons Book 2)

Summer Devotions: Part of the "Daily Devotion" Series (Seasons Book 3)

Fall Devotions: Part of the "Daily Devotion" Series (Seasons Book 4)

*All books are available on Amazon.

Made in the USA
Middletown, DE
14 July 2024

57279127R00130